THE IMPACT OF CIVILIAN EVACUATION IN THE SECOND WORLD WAR

THE IMPACT OF CIVILIAN EVACUATION IN THE SECOND WORLD WAR

TRAVIS L. CROSBY

CROOM HELM
London • Sydney • Dover, New Hampshire

Croom Helm Ltd, Provident House, Burrell Row,
Beckenham, Kent BR3 1AT

Croom Helm Australia Pty Ltd, Suite 4, 6th Floor,
64-76 Kippax Street, Surry Hills, NSW 2010, Australia

British Library Cataloguing in Publication Data

Crosby, Travis L.
The impact of civilian evacuation in the
Second World War.
1. World War, 1939-1945 – Evacuation of civilians
2. Children – Great Britain – History –
20th century
I. Title
940.53'161'0941 D809.G7

ISBN 0-7099-3433-5

Croom Helm, 51 Washington Street, Dover,
New Hampshire 03820, USA

Library of Congress Cataloging in Publication Data

Crosby, Travis L., 1936-
The impact of civilian evacuation in the second
world war.

Bibliography: p.
Includes index.
1. World war, 1939-1945–evacuation of civilians–
Great Britain. 2. World war, 1939-1945–Great Britain.
3. Great Britain–history–George VI, 1936-1952.
I. Title.
D809.G7C76 1986 940.53'159 85-29046
ISBN 0-7099-3433-5

Printed and bound in Great Britain
by Billing & Sons Limited, Worcester.

CONTENTS

Preface

Rummaging about in British record offices and libraries over the years, I've often encountered people who told stories of their own lives unrelated to my research into nineteenth century society and politics. A theme which appeared frequently among them was their wartime experiences. Especially interesting to me were stories from people of my own age who were school children during the second world war. What they remembered most vividly was the evacuation. To a North American, even at the distance of decades, it was a compelling story--hundreds of thousands of school children in movement across the countryside, seeking shelter from an expected aerial onslaught. Children were absent from their neighborhoods, schools, and parents for weeks or months at a time, some for the duration of the war.

As I heard these stories, I found myself almost imperceptibly searching for the historical significance of the evacuation. Surely a movement of such proportions had a direct social impact. How would parents and children have borne the separation? What were the origins and assumptions of evacuation planning? What did the government hope to gain by its evacuation policy? Was it a successful policy? This book is an attempt to answer these and like-minded questions: it charts the evolution of evacuation from its origins; examines its implementation; and finally suggests its possible effect upon post-war social planning in Britain. Because the evacuation disrupted the schooling of thousands of children, the book emphasizes its impact upon education.

Once I began my research in earnest, I discovered very few secondary works on the evacuation. R.M. Titmuss' Problems of Social Policy, a volume in the official history of the war, is the most complete. Its focus, however, is on the social problems which arose during the evacuation: very little is said about the background and implementation of the evacuation. Educational issues are omitted entirely: they were to have been included in a separate volume in the war history by Sophia Weitzman. This volume was never written.[1] Some of the material collected by Dr. Weitzman before her death in 1965 was used by Nigel Middleton in his A Place for Everyone; but there are only occasional references to the evacuation. P.H.J.H. Gosden's Education in the Second World War, although invaluable for the administrative side of things, also underplays the evacuation. Other secondary works, such as B.S. Johnson's The Evacuees, tend to be impressionistic and anecdotal, lacking in analytic content.

Wartime surveys which investigated the psychological and social conditions in reception area billets include the Barnett House Study Group's London Children in War-Time Oxford and Susan Isaacs' The Cambridge Evacuation Survey. Although they contain useful first-hand information about evacuees, they do not provide a sufficiently broad perspective for an understanding of the evacuation as a whole. They suffer, in addition, from methodological difficulties which plagued virtually every attempt to evaluate the effects of the evacuation upon children. Much of the psychological literature especially had inconsistent findings, driving one perplexed journal editor to plead for more reports, even if they covered identical groups of previous investigations.[2] Louise Despert, in noting a lack of systematic investigation among evacuation studies, reached the same conclusion.[3]

We are on surer ground, however, with the evidence that survives in the confidential memos and position papers of the various departments of state and local government involved in the evacuation, especially those of the Home Office, the Ministry of Health, the Board of Education, and the London County Council. Some of these records have been opened to the public only within the last decade. They candidly reveal the opinions of the planners and shed considerable light on conditions in the country-side during the evacuation. Significant collections of official papers are housed at the Greater London Record Office and the Public Record Office, Kew. Another important primary source are local newspapers, most conveniently located in the British Library's Newspaper Collection at Colindale. They furnish invaluable information about evacuation conditions through their reports of urban and district council meetings and summaries of cases from magistrates' courts. Opinions expressed in leading articles and letters to the editor are also useful. A final important contemporary source are diaries and first hand observations from evacuees, billeting officers, and householders during the evacuation. Some of these accounts are remarkably detailed and provide us with invaluable impressions of the evacuation. Collections of personal accounts may be found at the Greater London Record Office, the Mass Observation Archive at the University of Sussex, and the archives of the Imperial War Museum.

The major problem in using official papers, newspapers, and diaries is that they do not allow for easy quantification. Generalizations and conclusions reached in this book cannot therefore be based on numerate principles. This may seem a serious flaw in a study which attempts to examine the movement of several hundred thousand evacuees. In extenuation, I can only plead a recognition of the problem and an observation that each bit of evidence adds to the whole. If this is a circumstantial case, it is strongly so. I have tried to follow G.M. Young's advice to the historian to read until the dead speak. Ultimately, then, what follows must be an exercise in historical imagination. I offer here no apology, but rather an explanation of how I have worked. All in all, what we have said seems to make sense. But that is for the reader to judge.

I owe debts of gratitude to many for their help in making this book possible. First of all, my thanks to Wheaton College for sabbatical leave to begin research and writing; and to its provisions for scholarly activity throughout the years. The final stages of the book were immensely aided by the Meneely Professorship for the years 1983-85. As always, Nancy Shepardson and her staff at Wheaton have been essential to the completion of the manuscript.

My warmest thanks, too, for the generous aid given by the archivists, librarians, and staff at numerous research institutions in Britain, Canada, and the United States. Their hospitality makes scholarship a pleasure. I especially thank the British Library and its Newspaper Collection at Colindale; Churchill College, Cambridge; the Greater London Council History Library; the Greater London Record Office; the Imperial War Museum; the Mass Observation Archives at the University of Sussex; the National Union of Teachers; the Public Record Office at Kew; Trinity College, Cambridge; the University of London Library; and county record offices throughout Britain. In Canada, I am grateful to the archivist of MacMaster University. In the United States, most helpful to me were the New York Public Library; the libraries of Stanford University and the Hoover Institute; and, most particularly, the Sterling Library of Yale University.

I would also like to thank Faye Crosby, who gave much careful attention to the manuscript, and whose good sense and sound advice about writing are always invaluable. Dame Geraldine Aves, Philippa Brewster, Elizabeth Croll, Abigail Stewart, and Priscilla Thurber gave additional help at various stages of the manuscript. Their encouragement and timely assistance were crucial. I dedicate this book to Timothy Andrews Crosby: my hope is that he may never know of an evacuation at first hand.

NOTES

1. M. Davies, 'Education in the Second World War: The Preparation of an Official History', _Journal of Educational Administration and History_, vol. VIII, no. 1 (January 1976), pp. 51-55.

2. C.W. Valentine, 'Editorial Note on Evacuation Investigations', _British Journal of Educational Psychology_, vol. XI (1941), p. 127; for a complete bibliography of wartime psychological studies during the evacuation, see Katherine M. Wolf, 'Evacuation of Children in Wartime', _Psychoanalytic Study of the Child_, vol. I (1945), pp. 389-404.

3. J. Louise Despert, _Preliminary Report on Children's Reactions to the War_ (n.p., 1942).

CHAPTER ONE

Introduction

The early days of World War II will always be associated with the sight of British school children marching raggedly to train depots as they left the vulnerable cities of London, Liverpool, Glasgow, or Sheffield in the face of threatened bombing raids by the Luftwaffe. In the four days following 1 September 1939, several hundred thousand children were evacuated to relatively safe provincial towns and rural villages.

From that time to this, the evacuation has remained a part of wartime legend. Contemporary accounts of the evacuation emphasized the courage of the evacuees and the sacrifices of the rural hosts who took them in. Norah Baring's _A Friendly Hearth_ tells how the author took the tenancy of a large house in Wales and filled it with evacuee children. William Busby's _Our Evacuees_ offers a no less engaging story. There were also accounts of the adventures of overseas evacuees. Meta Maclean served as a host on what she called _The Singing Ship_ which bore away five hundred evacuees on a 20,000 mile round about voyage to Australia. _The Young Ambassadors_ by Angela Pelham describes her life as an evacuee to the United States.[1] These books and all others like them portray the evacuation as an outgrowth of a broadly based humanitarian movement securing the safety of Britain's children from the terrors of war.

The evacuation was also widely believed to have been an opportunity for bringing together diverse and conflicting strands in British society. As a contemporary writer put it, evacuation was 'one of the boldest experiments in the social history of this century' because of its 'rapid and enforced breaking down of the barrier between the town child and his country host'.[2] The Oxford Group, better known as Moral Re-Armament, published a pamphlet with the message that evacuation could 'unite the nation in a new responsibility for the welfare of its children, and provide a doorway to great and beneficient social changes'--if, of course, the precepts of Moral Re-Armament were widely accepted.[3] More radical opinion thought the evacuation could promote a democratic movement leading to the completion of social reforms, in abeyance since Lloyd George's day.[4] It would work this way. The intrusion of disadvantaged evacuees into affluent rural settings would give a salutary shock to complacent countrymen: their consciences thus pricked would spur them to advocate social legislation. This view of the evacuation has influenced historians of our own day. Arthur Marwick has written that evacuation was one of the most important phenomena of the war because it 'brought to middle- and upper-class households a consciousness for the first time of the deplorable conditions endemic in the rookeries and warrens which still existed in Britain's great industrial cities, and so, among the articulate few, aroused a new sense of social reform'.[5] According to this interpretation, the evacuation played its part in breaking down historic class distinctions during the war.

How accurate are these descriptions of the evacuation? How well did the urban evacuees interact with their rural hosts? And most importantly, how realistic were the hopes that the evacuation would initiate among rural householders a renewed sense of reform and responsibility for the ills of society? Courage and self-sacrifice there certainly was in abundance. Many foster parents provided congenial billets for their wartime guests, who adapted quickly to their new surroundings once the initial homesickness had passed. Considerable numbers of evacuees and foster parents grew fond of one another. Some evacuees kept up their contacts with rural householders long after the war. Visits to wartime 'aunts' and 'uncles' have figured prominently in holiday plans until very recent days. For thousands, evacuation memories have been agreeable ones. But well adjusted evacuees are not the subject of this study. If all evacuees had encountered only pleasantness in the countryside, our story of the evacuation would be very short indeed.

The real significance of the evacuation lies among those evacuees who discovered hostility and dislike in the reception areas. We shall review evidence which demonstrates that the juxtaposition of urban evacuees and their more affluent rural hosts was far more discordant than contemporaries believed. Writers of that time and later commentators have assumed too readily that the mere mixture of people from divergent backgrounds would be harmonious and beneficial. But students of social psychology know that this is a naive point of view: group interaction has as much chance of alienating groups as it has of changing attitudes and beliefs about one another.[6] As we shall see, conflicts and clashes were severe enough and numerous enough to have threatened the entire evacuation program more than once.

The fault was not one-sided. An observer of evacuation failures in the affluent Liverpool suburbs of Blundellands and West Kirby thought the problems were due equally to 'piggish habits' on the one hand and 'selfish intolerance' on the other.[7] No doubt some evacuees were beyond the pale. The antics of the odious Connollys in Evelyn Waugh's Put Out more Flags had the ring of truth for numerous rural hosts. Yet as the weeks of evacuation went forward, it became increasingly clear that the evacuees were becoming the victims of the evacuation. Personality clashes, religious hatreds, differing habits of speech and behavior, and old-fashioned xenophobia all played a role. Most important of all were three distinct, yet complimentary, attitudes among reception area inhabitants. These attitudes were rooted in the assumptions of Social Darwinism; in racial prejudice, especially anti-Semitism;and in the distrust bred of class divisions within British society.

The influence of Social Darwinism is difficult to trace. The subtle ways in which its doctrines worked upon the minds of government officials and public alike are only now coming to light.[8] There seems little doubt, however, about the extent of organized Social Darwinism in the early decades of this century. This usually took the form of eugenic education societies. Because eugenics held that poverty was caused by faults of character and personal deficiencies of the poor, preventive programs designed to improve social conditions were thought ineffective. Concerned eugenicists advocated segregation and sterilization of the unfit, or other types of punitive and restrictive measures to 'ginger up' the poor. Membership of the eugenic societies were often drawn from those scientists, educators, and doctors who believed that the population of Britain was threatened by 'tainted stock' and that only energetic state action could prevent a racial disaster. Sir Cyril Burt, the foremost psychologist of his day (and whose work is now largely discredited), was a founding member of the Liverpool branch of the Eugenics Education Society. Neville Chamberlain was enrolled in the Birmingham branch, as was George Auden, appointed the School Medical Officer in Birmingham in 1908. Indeed, the medical profession played an especially important role in the growing public acceptance of eugenicism after World War I. Medical conferences were increasingly dominated by the eugenic debate, as the pages of the _Lancet_ attest. Significant, too, in disseminating the ideas of eugenics among the scientific community was the journal _Nature_, whose editor in the 1920's was Sir Richard Gregory--an editor also of _School World_ and the _Journal of Education_. The drift of their argument can be caught by an article appearing in _Nature_ in 1924. It claimed that intelligence testing had proven 'a large proportion of the slum populations consists of..."morons"--that is, of mental defectives.... These people are lacking not only in intelligence but also in self-control, which is the basis of morality, and they reproduce recklessly'.[9]

Ideas such as these had a noticeable impact upon government officials. A report issued jointly by the Board of Education and the Board of Control in 1929 entitled _Mental Deficiency_ suggested that feeble-mindedness had doubled in recent decades. Two years later, in 1931, a sterilization bill was introduced in the House of Commons but, to the discouragement of the eugenicists, it failed. More important for our purposes was the impact of eugenics upon evacuation. Because evacuees originated largely from the slums and poorer districts of the great cities, they were thought to be feckless and irresponsible. Reception area officials, including school medical officers, acted accordingly in assuming that evacuees must be taken in hand and carefully managed.

A second reason for hostility against evacuees--and one that is directly related to Social Darwinism--was the growth of anti-Semitism in the 1920's and 1930's. Recent studies have shown that anti-Semitism in Britain reached far beyond such fascist leaders and publicists as Oswald Mosley and General J.F.C. Fuller and their followers.[10] Anti-Jewish remarks and behavior was shared by street hooligans, tradesmen, Oxford dons, and politicians. One estimate has it that three-quarters of the British population held unfavorable attitudes toward Jews.[11] Readers of diaries of the time will find ample evidence of anti-Semitic feelings: Chips Channon and Harold Nicholson were not the least of these--although Nicholson had the grace to be embarrassed by his prejudice. Attitudes so readily accepted in all ranks of society could not but affect the evacuation planner. Some poorer sections of Britain's largest cities, especially the East End of London, had a large number of Jewish residents, thus providing the planners with a specific focus for their latent Social Darwinism and anti-Semitism. As the planners thought through the displacement of urban Jewish residents in wartime, their prejudices made it easier to think of city crowds as an abstraction, as objects merely to be controlled and directed in times of emergency. Once Jewish evacuees were in the countryside, they again met prejudice. The evacuees were regarded as exotic, foreign, and un-English--and not to be tolerated.

The third important source of hostility against the evacuees, and one that gave shape and substance to the others, was, broadly speaking, a suspicion and distrust of one class for another. Traditionally, upper class notions of the lower class role in the state was based upon the belief in the necessity of upper class domination. Lower classes had to be kept in their place--content if possible; but, above all, orderly. Once individual lower class members had attained sufficient property or status, only then could they participate fully in society. Any national emergency could threaten this orderly and hierarchical view of social progress. The uncertainties of wartime could be particularly dangerous. New weaponry, developed during World War I, brought an added dimension to the problems of public order. The rapid deployment of high speed aircraft against the home front could strike against the very structure of society. In the face of multiple air attacks, the tendency to panic among the poor was considered inevitable. Living in substandard housing, in overcrowded conditions and without transport, workers would be trapped in the cities. As the toll of dead and wounded mounted, morale would break. To prevent mass panic, an evacuation scheme was imperative. As is obvious, however, evacuation meant evacuation mostly of the poor. One evacuation planner made this plain: 'it is not for the readers of "The Times", he wrote, 'but the working people...for whom our evacuation policy must be planned'.[12] Only workers needed for essential wartime jobs would remain in the cities: their wives and children, less important to the war effort and the least reliable in times of stress, would be priority cases for the evacuation scheme. Middle and upper class citizens, it was believed, would calmly shift for themselves.

The class assumptions of evacuation planners should not be surprising. Only a handful of military authorities and the civil servants responsible for evacuation planning in the 1920's and 1930's had working class origins. Most came from privileged backgrounds. Working class behavior and attitudes were unfamiliar to them. This was especially true of the higher civil servants who had gone to the preferred schools and universities. Born in late Victorian times and now reaching the peak of their careers, they lived comfortably in Hampstead, Wimbledon, or the Home Counties. They often belonged to one or more of the prestigious London clubs and mixed socially with people of similar professions such as lawyers and politicians. They were far removed from the daily life of urban working families whose members were to be evacuated in wartime. This is not to suggest that civil servants would inherently be unable to make sensible decisions relating to evacuees simply because most evacuees were working class. Nor were civil servants necessarily divorced from issues of concern to the working class. Indeed, one estimation of political preferences among the higher civil servants in the 1930's placed them left of center. [13] Nevertheless, it was difficult for them, lacking first hand knowledge, to understand fully some of the issues involved in separating children from their closely-knit working class families.

Complementary to the civil service view were the dominant conservative ideas among those who held public office. The composition of the governments of the 1930's, invariably conservative, reinforced the sense that traditional policies were wisest to pursue in disordered times. Like the civil servants, conservative ministers had unstated assumptions about the working class which shaped their evacuation policy as it shaped their social and economic policies. Yet conservative ministers held a naive view that once the evacuation had begun, the countryside, as a matter of patriotic duty, would welcome lower class evacuees with open arms. The government's miscalculation was evident from the first days of evacuation in September, 1939. A substantial number of rural hosts rejected the evacuees. Complaints from villages and towns were numerous and sustained. There were reports of dirty and verminous children, of bedwetters, or hooligans. The countryside had been invaded by undesirables. On the face of it, these were complaints of appearance and behavior; but a closer examination reveals a deeper truth. Social stratification at the local level was sabotaging the evacuation.

This would not have been surprising to a student of rural England. Sociological studies have shown how readily villagers group themselves into classes.[14] The criteria for class divisions vary, of course: they may be based upon education, occupation, or family background. These criteria were not usually known about evacuees, and the natural tendency of villagers was to assign them to specific classes based upon first impressions. Often, the scruffy appearance of evacuees at the door would tell rural hosts more than enough about their wartime guests. Because the evacuees were strangers, moreover, there was a probable tendency to underestimate class ranking: alien speech; unaccustomed dress; distinct ways of sitting or standing or eating would cause evacuees to be placed within a lower class grouping than evacuees themselves would ascribe. This was doubtless galling to those evacuees and their families who considered themselves at the upper end of the working class structure; for within the working class itself, there were sharp gradations.[15] Class attributions of evacuees were not confined to the villages. The inhabitants of substantial provincial towns thought as readily in terms of class. In Banbury, for example, traditional views of social acceptability made Banburians consider as foreigners immigrants from only a few miles distance.[16] An influx of hundreds of evacuees into private homes and neighborhoods from far away towns and cities would confuse and threaten the accepted social order.

Once middle and upper class hosts, or even the respectable working class with social pretensions, had 'placed' their evacuees, they were aloof, probably condescending, and occasionally rude and offensive to the evacuees. They certainly did not wish to have the evacuees in their own homes. Even after the war, bitter memories remained in some reception areas. In Stevenage, Hertfordshire, plans for a New Town site evoked strong opposition in 1946 because it was assumed that immigrants would come from the East End or other overcrowded London areas. It reminded Stevenage residents too vividly of their two thousand wartime evacuees. At a protest meeting, a former billeting officer who had substantial contacts with hundreds of evacuees during the war, including twelve in his own house, 'was sure the people of Stevenage never wanted to see them again'.[17] Antagonism to the evacuees was especially marked among what were termed the 'well-to-do-'--the most affluent and respectable country hosts. Anecdotal evidence may be confirmed by government reports: the wealthy shunned the evacuees; the poor cottager welcomed them.

Unsatisfactory billeting conditions in the autumn of 1939 drove large numbers of evacuees back to their urban homes. By mid-November 1939, the rate of 'drift back', as the government called it, was more than 6000 weekly to London alone. By the summer of 1940, half of all London evacuees had left the reception areas. Only in periods of extreme danger did evacuees venture again into the countryside. This occurred twice more in the war--during the London blitz of late summer 1940 and in the flying bomb attacks of 1944. Each time, the pattern was repeated: after the immediate danger passed, evacuees left the reception areas.

Clearly the evacuees who went into the countryside after 1939 did so reluctantly. 'Once evaucated, twice shy' was an East End maxim early in 1940. The evacuees did not conform to the government's expectations. Indeed, what is most striking about the evacuation is that thousands of women and children--and their husbands and fathers--should have willingly put themselves at risk by remaining in the cities when provisions had been made by the government to offer them safety in the countryside. Their actions had an important consequence: it seriously disrupted the government's civil defense policy. Yet the government was reluctant to abandon its reliance upon the concept of voluntarism: it rejected, for example, compulsory billeting. Instead, it began a campaign of persuasion in the countryside to improve householder attitude toward the evacuees. The campaign failed, as we shall see.

The most important effect of this massive wartime migration between urban ghettoes and the counties was the opportunity it gave for a process of social comparison on a grand scale. Tens of thousands of working class families, leaving their accustomed friends and narrowly circumscribed neighborhoods were brought face to face with class prejudice in some form. Time and again, they bumped against a patronizing attitude, a subtle disapproval, or outright dislike. For many evacuees it was their first contact with the privileged life of a wealthy community. By expanding the incidents of class antagonisms during the war, the evacuation helped create the post-war demand for a removal of class restrictions. It was not that the evacuation opened the eyes of the middle and upper class to the deplorable conditions of the many, as some historians have argued. To the contrary, the evacuation opened the eyes of the working class to the advantages of the few. This gives point to Paul Addison's observation that the foundations of political power began to shift leftward as early as 1940.[18] The introduction of labour ministers into the cabinet, the dissemination of social democratic ideals over the BBC and in the army, and the emphasis on 'fair shares' symbolized by the ration book all no doubt played a part. The premier event, however, was the evacuation. It was the earliest wartime experience for the population that placed Britain, in Addison's words, on the road to 1945.

NOTES

1. Norah Baring, *A Friendly Hearth* (London, 1946); William H. Busby, *Our Evacuees: A Reminiscence* (London, 1941); Angela Pelham, *The Young Ambassadors* (London, 1944); Meta MacLean, *The Singing Ship: An Odyssey of Evacuee Children* (Sydney, 1941).

2. Alfred H. Body, *Children in Flight* (London, 1940).

3. Philip Leon, *et al.*, 'Evacuation: A National Opportunity' (1940).

4. A.D.K. Owen, 'The Great Evacuation', *The Political Quarterly*, Vol. XI (1940).

5. Arthur Marwick, *War and Social Change in the Twentieth Century* (London 1974), p. 157; and Marwick, *The Home Front: The British and the Second World War* (London, 1976), p. 75.

6. See, for example, Yehuda Amir, 'Contact Hypothesis in Ethnic Relations', *Psychological Bulletin*, Vol. 71, No. 5 (May 1969), pp. 319-42.

7. Imperial War Museum, Norman F. Ellison, 'War on the Home Front', memoirs in typescript, DS/Misc/49.

8. Much of the information in this paragraph may be found in R.A. Lowe, 'Eugenicists, Doctors and the Quest for National Efficiency: An Educational Crusade, 1900-1939', _History of Education_, Vol. 8, No. 4 (1979), pp. 293-306. See also Greta Jones, 'Eugenics and Social Policy Between the Wars', _The Historical Journal_, Vol. 25, No. 3 (1982), pp. 717-28.

9. E. MacBride, 'Social Biology and Birth Control', _Nature_, Vol. 113 (31 May 1924), p. 774; quoted in Gary Wersky, _The Visible College: The Collective Biography of British Scientific Socialists of the 1930's_ (New York, 1978), p. 42.

10. See Gisela C. Lebzelter, _Political Anti-Semitism in England, 1918-1939_ (London, 1978) and Colin Holmes, _Anti-Semitism in British Society, 1876-1939_ (London, 1979).

11. H.J. Eysenck, _Uses and Abuses of Psychology_ (Edinburgh, 1953), p. 261; quoted by Lebzelter, _Political Anti-Semitism in England_.

12. Public Record Office HO 45/16634.

13. Information about the civil service is taken from R.K. Kelsall, _Higher Civil Servants in Britain_ (London, 1955) and H.E. Dale, _The Higher Civil Service of Great Britain_ (Oxford, 1941).

14. See, for example, W.M. Williams, _The Sociology of an English Village: Gosforth_ (London, 1956).

15. As Robert Roberts reminds us in his _The Classic Slum_ (Manchester, 1971), Ch. 1.

16. Margaret Stacy, _Tradition and Change: A Study of Banbury_ (Oxford, 1960).

17. Harold Orlands, _Stevenage: A Sociological Study of a New Town_ (London, 1952), p. 161-2.

18. Paul Addison, _The Road to 1945: British Politics and the Second World War_ (London, 1975).

CHAPTER TWO

Evolution of a Policy

Evacuation planning grew out of the experiences of the 1914-1918 war. For the first time in its history, Britain lost its island advantage over a hostile continental power. The traditional Channel defense could be neutralized by an opponent with a strong air force. When enemy aircraft appeared for the first time over English soil, it was no doubt an inauspicious beginning: a single German bomb broke some windows near Dover Castle on Christmas Eve, 1914. But a bombing raid over London a few months later gave a better display of air power. A ton of bombs from a German airship killed seven and injured thirty-five, mostly in the East End. In the following twelve months, Zeppelin attacks in Britain were fairly frequent. The worst single incident of the war occurred in a daylight raid on 13 June 1917 when fourteen German _Gothas_--twin-engined air-craft--bombed the City of London and the East End killing 162 and injuring 426. There were in all 103 German bombing raids on British soil, about equally divided between air ships and fixed wing aircraft. They dropped 300 tons causing 4820 casualties including 1413 fatalities.[1] It took little imagination to see that improved aircraft would greatly enhance the destructive power of a potential enemy.

Protection against enemy bombers could most simply be achieved by active defense; that is, by shooting them down. But some bombers were bound to get through, and here passive civil defense had to bear the burden. Unless some feasible plan were devised, military authorities believed that in any future war, enemy air craft would devastate the great industrial cities, sending thousands of terrified people into panic-stricken flight. With forty percent of its population concentrated in its six largest urban centers, Britain seemed particularly vulnerable. Deep shelters against bombing attacks was one possible defense, but these were costly and would not in any case alleviate the problem of panic. Crowds of people huddled together underground in retreat from a rain of bombs above was an unacceptable vision for the authorities. An orderly movement of civilians from likely targets was a better solution. By dispersing the population, death and injuries could be substantially reduced and panic minimized.

Official civil defense planning, emphasizing evacuation, was initially taken up by the Committee of Imperial Defense. The CID was an authoritative body whose recommendations were usually made directly to the cabinet.[2] It had a complete supporting secretariat and the power to create special standing committees on which ministers of government often sat. In 1924, the CID created a sub-committee to review civil defense policy. Formally known as the Air Raid Precautions (ARP) Sub-Committee, it consisted of representatives from the Ministry of Health, the Office of Works, and the three service departments. Two eminent senior civil servants were its principal officers. The secretary was Sir Maurice Hankey, who held every important secretariat within the civil service, including the Cabinet, the CID, and the clerkship of the Privy Council. The chairman was Sir John Anderson, at that time Permanent Under Secretary of State for the Home Department. Anderson served nearly eight years as chairman of the ARP Sub-Committee and was destined to become the most important government official in the development of a civil defense policy in the inter-war years.[3] Before coming to the Home Office, Anderson had a diverse and distinguished career: he had served in the Colonial Office, the Ministry of Health, and the Board of Inland Revenue. Early on, he had gained a reputation as an imperturbable man on the spot. He was awarded a KGCB for his work as Under Secretary for Ireland during the time of the troubles from 1920-22. A dour

Scotsman, Anderson was never at ease in social gatherings. It was said that in ordinary conversation, he often spoke like an official minute and was reputed to read nothing but Blue Books. But there was no doubt about his administrative talents. Anderson believed that civil defense ought not be centralized in one department lest an emergency create an intolerable burden and involve the risk of a breakdown. The ARP Sub-Committee's role, as he saw it, was to devise a means of coordinating the various agencies responsible for civil defense. He also firmly believed that voluntarism and persuasion, rather than government legislation, should play a significant role in implementing a civil defense program.

In these early days, the Sub-Committee worked in secrecy. If its deliberations became known, Anderson feared the public would think the government was preparing for war.[4] The Sub-Committee also apparently believed the information it gathered was too disquieting to be publicized. Because passive civil defense policy was predicated on the size and strength of continental air forces, much of the Sub-Committee's attention during the late 1920's was given to estimates of the likely scale of enemy attacks. Data and observations from the Air Staff provided the basis for its calculations. Overall, the Air Staff's estimates were alarming. They projected that an enemy would exert maximum strength at the beginning of a war and that London would be the main target. As much as 200 tons of bombs would be dropped in the first day, 150 tons in the second, and 100 tons on each successive day for the first month. (It will be remembered that only 300 tons were dropped in all of the first world war.) Projected casualties would be even more devastating: 5000 casualties the first day; 3750 the second day; and 2500 daily thereafter.[5] In the light of these estimates, it is not surprising that the Sub-Committee shared the military concern about the effects of extensive bombing on civilian morale. To give more attention to morale and to the role that evacuation would play in the larger picture of civil defense, Anderson's Sub-Committee appointed its own sub-committee.

The Evacuation Sub-Committee first met in March 1931, chaired by Sir Charles Hipwood of the Board of Trade. Wing Commander E.J. Hodsoll served as secretary and the following year replaced Hipwood as chairman. Hankey, the CID secretary, also took an active role in the Evacuation Sub-Committee's deliberations. The minutes of the meeting reveal the unquestioned assumption that evacuation was necessary because certain elements of the civilian population were liable to panic. As Hipwood put it, once an aerial bombardment had begun, there would probably be 'an almost irresistible impulse to get to ground or to bolt'.[6] This would most likely happen, he believed, among the inhabitants of the poorer sections of large cities. Other authorities coming before the Sub-Committee substantiated Hipwood's opinion. Major Tomlin of the Metropolitan Police Force relayed to the Committee information from one of his Police Superintendents who had been stationed in London's East End during the first world war. The Superintendent claimed that he had detected panic, especially among the Jewish population, when the air raid sirens had sounded. A lengthy bombardment upon 'this type of population' would cause them to 'be driven mad with fright', the superintendent concluded. He also mentioned that the native English had taken comparatively little notice of air raid alerts and had gone about their business undisturbed. Later discussions made it clear that at least in the mind of some committee members, an equation was made between 'Jewish' and 'foreign'. In Hipwood's words, 'the foreign element' may present 'a rather special problem'.[7] A secret CID report confirmed the necessity for evacuating citizens in poor areas because they were 'likely to form a most unstable element--an element very susceptible to panic. The worst of all will, doubtless, be found in the East End, and those who had experience in the last war will recall the appalling scenes which occurred in this area'.[8]

Following the belief of its sub-committees that civil defense was largely a matter of crowd control and the prevention of panic, the CID recommended that the primary responsibility for civil defense be placed in the Home Office, the ministry in charge of the police forces of the country. Thus, an Air Raid Precautions Department became a tenth administrative division in the Home Office in 1935. Wing Commander Hodsoll became its head with the rank of Assistant Secretary of State. Hodsoll was a natural choice. Before he became involved with civil defense work, he had had a distinguished career with the RAF. Shortly after his schooling at Christ's Hospital, Hodsoll joined the Royal Naval Air Service where he served during the first world war, rising to Commander at the British sea plan base in Alexandria. In 1923 he was at the Staff College, Camberley, and in 1925 with the RAF in India. In 1929 he had organized the evacuation of British civilians from Kabul during the Afghan rebellion of that year.

Under Hodsoll the newly created ARP Department continued the tradition of secrecy in civil defense planning. The Department collected data, some of it from foreign sources, in establishing the relative place of Britain in civil defense preparations. It conducted bombing experiments, tested respirators, and opened an anti-Gas School at Falfield in Gloucestershire. Hodsoll soon realized, however, that an ARP program could not be kept completely secret: the bombing experiments themselves were bound to attract public attention. Eventually, too, the full participation of local officials would be necessary to the implementation of civil defense. An early step toward public disclosure was taken in July 1935 when an ARP circular was issued to local government authorities by the Home Office. It invited local authorities to cooperate in establishing a national defense scheme. This was not a statutory command: officials were asked to devise schemes voluntarily. In late 1935 Hodsoll visited twenty-five local authorities throughout the country to encourage their participation in ARP work. His minutes provide a useful summary of the state of ARP at the time.[9]

Hodsoll discovered there was considerable opposition to the government's proposals. Jealousies between some units of local government about ARP responsibility had developed. Officials occasionally refused to co-operate on pacifist grounds: they believed that civil defense planning would create a war psychology. One mayor of a large northern city thought the best civil defense was unilateral disarmament. Needless to say, Hodsoll had little sympathy with what he called 'that queer mood' of pacifism.[10] A more serious difficulty was the reluctance of local authorities to assume the cost of ARP work. Because ARP was a part of national defense, local officials believed the government ought to bear the full cost. They feared civil defense would either push up the rates or force a reduction in social services to meet civil defense charges.

The government held that civil defense was a natural addition to local authorities' statutory duties of public order, fire protection and the like. Civil defense should be merely grafted onto existing units of local government. This had the advantage of administative simplicity. In addition, it accorded with the conservative government's treasury view of strict economy. Insofar as possible, the government hoped to base its civil defense program, as a spokesman put it, 'upon the twofold base of self-help and voluntary endeavor'.[11] It was a point often re-iterated by Sir John Anderson. Civil defense, he believed, was essentially 'the business of helping the people to protect themselves'; it was 'a local service' and not a 'fourth arm of defense'.[12]

The government's claims did not persuade the local authorities. And, because civil defense was largely voluntary, they dragged their heels. In late 1937, the government was finally forced to bring forward legislation compelling the creation of local civil defense schemes. Debated in the House of Commons in November, the Air Raid Precautions Bill was the most important public discussion on civil defense yet heard.[13] Sir Samuel Hoare, Home Secretary under Chamberlain, made the case for the Bill claiming that the government's civil defense program was well advanced but that more needed doing. He proposed an extension of the existing duties of local authorities as the most desirable means of completing the program. Arguing against the government, Herbert Morrison emphasized the need for administrative efficiency. Although his passion for order could never have been guessed from his untidy appearance, Morrison was in fact efficient, assiduous, and methodical. His brand of socialism was less ideological than practical:

for Morrison the competent solution to knotty problems was the highest form of state service.[14] During the debate he argued that local authorities did not want autonomy in matters of civil defense: they wanted to act as agents of the state. It was the only way to 'clean-cut, quick, decisive administration'.[15] Morrison demanded a thorough and detailed government plan, with the government bearing the full cost of the program. As front bench spokesman for the labour party, and leader of the London County Council, Morrison's views carried weight.

Other opposition speakers fastened on what they considered a serious omission in the government's proposed bill: there was no specific mention of evacuation. Dr. Haden Guest, Labour member of Islington North, believed that evacuation should be the 'first consideration' of the ministry. He pointed out that the poorer areas of the larger cities with their narrow streets, tall buildings and overcrowded populations could not be adequately served by a shelter policy alone. The Labour member for Glasgow (St. Rollox), William Leonard, also made a strong plea for a government evacuation scheme on similar grounds. His constituency included Cowcaddens, a notorious slum district, where it would be impossible to construct adequate shelters. Evacuation would be the only sensible policy. Even Conservative backbenchers agreed that evacuation should be taken into account in any legislative measures on civil defense. It was in fact an inexplicable lapse on the part of the government, given the many previous years' work on evacuation. Pressed on several sides, Hoare brought forward a few weeks later an additional clause which specifically made evacuation a repsonsibility of ARP planning by local authorities. The bill as amended was given the royal assent on 22 December 1937.

Even with legislative encouragement, the problems in planning civil defense and evacuation were not easily resolved. Question time in parliament over the next few months revealed that implementation of the ARP bill was proceeding very slowly: Geoffrey Lloyd, Under Secretary for the Home Office, often gave lame or vague answers about the progress of local ARP schemes. On 19

May 1938 he admitted that local authorities 'in spite of copious memoranda issued by the Home Office' were finding the task difficult.[16] This made public what the civil service had known privately for months. In the Home Office papers a memo by Wilfrid Eady of the ARP Department dated 26 February 1938 observed that local authorities had been bewildered by the amount of advice and exhortation they had received since the passage of the 1937 bill. Confused by the complexity of the duties put upon them by the act, many authorities simply did not know where to begin.[17] On 26 May 1938, one week after Lloyd's damaging admission, Hoare announced to the House of Commons that a parliamentary committee of four, chaired by Sir John Anderson - now a member of the House of Commons - had been appointed to bring evacuation 'under full review'.[18]

Anderson's metamorphosis from civil servant to parliamentarian had been dramatically rapid. He was recently returned at a by-election for the Scottish Universities, the seat falling vacant upon the death of Ramsay MacDonald in November 1937. Anderson only agreed on the candidacy with the understanding that he would be an independent member of parliament. His civil service background had conditioned him, as he said in his election address, against becoming a party man at this stage of his career. Anderson's relative freedom from the constraints of party gave him an advantage over the more committed political approaches to the question of evacuation: he was bound neither to the voluntarism of the government (though he leaned in this direction) nor to the socialist arguments of Morrison. If free of party dictates, Anderson's attitude as a member of the new evacuation committee nevertheless was at first unchanged from his earlier years as chairman of the CID sub-committee. In his initial address to the new committee, he charged them with devising methods of avoiding panic among civilians.[19] To Anderson's credit, however, he soon realized that the parliamentary debates had placed the evacuation policy on a different plane. It had become clear from the debates that standards of living and slum conditions must shape to some degree any evacuation policy. The urban poor, once evacuated, had to have minimal provisions of care. To the original concerns of public order, evacuation planners had now to add educational and social issues.

The formation of the Anderson Committee accelerated the growing debate on evacuation policy. At the London County Council, a young and energetic Assistant Education Officer, G.A.N. Lowndes, wrote his superior suggesting that teachers be included in the membership of the Anderson Committee.[20] Lowndes' letter was given a favorable reading by Morrison in his capacity as head of the LCC. Soon Frederick Mander, Secretary of the National Union of Teachers, was enlisted. Within a few weeks, Lowndes, Mander, and E.M. Rich, Chief Education Officer at the LCC, met with the Anderson Committee. Thus began a powerful alliance between the government evacuation planners and the London County Council. The very size of the LCC, which was responsible for the largest school district in Britain, and its proximity to the centers of authority, assured it of a hearing. From their bastion at County Hall, LCC educational officers made continued sorties across the Thames to Whitehall and parliament.

LCC concerns were several. At the time of the appointment of the Anderson Committee, such fundamental issues as numbers, categories, and priority of departure of evacuees were undecided. The planners had merely assumed that all but essential workers would be removed before the attacks began. The LCC believed strongly that children and mothers should be evacuated first. If necessary, other sections of the population should be held back until the children were safe. Further, the children should go out in cohesive school units, led by their teachers who had the trust of parents. The LCC believed, too, that the children should be billeted in private homes in the countryside, rather than in special camps or hostels. Otherwise, teachers must act *in loco parentis*. As Mander testified before the Anderson Committee, the use of private billets would make it possible 'to place some responsibility upon the occupier of the house to look after the children. To this extent the teachers would become relieved of the impracticable task of looking after the children twenty-four hours a day'.[21] It was a recommendation that would return to haunt teacher and pupil alike.

The LCC's influence was reflected in the Anderson Committee's final report.[22] It gave school children and mothers with infants first claim to transport and billeting facilities. The idea of private billets pleased the government because it cost far less than constructing special camps for the evacuees: only a small billeting allowance (initially 8s 6d a week) given the rural hosts for each evacuee would be necessary. The Committee recommended school by school departure from designated evacuation areas to specified reception areas. So-called neutral areas, where neither bombs nor evacuees were expected, would be left undisturbed. Depending on their classification--evacuation, reception, or neutral---local authorities with Home Office guidance could at last begin systematic planning. In addition, the Committee abandoned the secrecy which had characterized evacuation planning. ARP and the evacuation scheme were to be given extensive publicity.

By their work the Anderson Committee established the basic principles on which the evacuation of September 1939 was eventually carried out.[23] The Committee had held twenty-five meetings, many of them lengthy. They had examined fifty-seven witnesses, and representatives from twenty-six government and private organizations, including the various political parties, the railways, military authorities, and teachers' organizations. In casting a wide net, the Committee drew upon sources never before taken into account by evacuation planners. Thus, they helped to assure a large measure of public support.

As the summer days of 1938 lengthened, a sense of urgency grew among civil defense planners. The diplomatic sky was darkening. With one eye on the deteriorating relations with Germany, the Anderson Committee rushed through the final stages of its report, completing it on 26 July 1938. The report was given immediately to the Home Secretary. As August slipped past, evacuation planners grew worried. Nothing further was heard from Whitehall. By late August, County Hall was plainly alarmed. From 22 August until 12

September, Lowndes rang the Home Office almost daily. To jog them along, he deposited with the ARP Department an improvised London evacuation plan.[24] Only on 15 September, the very eve of Chamberlain's flight to Berchtesgaden at the height of the Munich crisis, was the Anderson Report finally given to the CID for review. The CID decided to delay the publication of the Report, recommending instead that it be used internally in an abbreviated form as a guide for evacuation.

In the final two weeks in September, there was feverish activity among responsible evacuation authorities.[25] Meetings between the Home Secretary, LCC representatives, and representatives of the London Passenger Transport Board were quickly called. Educational Officers of the LCC held hurried conferences with heads of schools to solicit opinions and advice. At one of these meetings it was suggested children might cycle out of the danger zones. This recommendation demonstrated the rudimentary level of evacuation planning as it then was. The immense logistical problems in moving hundreds of thousands of women and children into a largely unprepared countryside created confusion and a palpable sense of panic among the planners---perhaps a suitably ironic response. By 26 September, a rough evacuation scheme for London was pieced together. The LCC, led by Morrison, urged the Home Office to set evacuation in motion, but it refused on the grounds that the reception areas were unprepared. Fortunately, by 1 October the threat of war had passed and evacuation was unnecessary.

The sense of relief among evacuation planners when the crisis receded may easily be imagined. But relief was quickly replaced by chagrin at the lack of preparedness. Critical post-mortems in the press put the blame directly on the Home Office for delaying the evacuation program.[26] Consternation among local authorities was also evident. A member of the Wiltshire County Council who had attended a planning session in London in September wrote that he found the officials at the Home Office 'in a very panicky condition with regard to the evacuation of civilians...'.[27] The clerk of the

Gloucestershire County Council condemned the evaucation scheme as 'fundamentally unsound'.[28] A well-connected member of the Shropshire Federation of Women's Institutes wrote the clerk of the Salop County Council in October of a recent trip to London where she heard on all sides 'how lamentable' the evacuation planning had been--'a complete muddle and everything that was bad'.[29]

Opposition political parties quickly took advantage of their opportunity. In the House of Commons, Morrison moved a vote of censure against the government. He energetically criticized the government's record on civil defense in a powerful and effective speech. He demanded to know 'what the Government have been doing ever since 1931'. More specifically, he charged that the government 'had no policy of evacuation when the crisis emerged'.[30] Criticism was not confined to partisan voices. Lowndes believed that the Home Office had been slow from the first on evacuation policy. Quoting an inside source at the ARP Department, he wrote to E.M. Rich at the LCC that ARP officials had 'a hole and corner secretiveness' unlike any other in the civil service.[31] Rich himself complained of snubs from the Home Office during the crisis.[32] Among senior civil servants there was a talk of a policy failure. In a letter marked 'secret' to Sir Alexander Maxwell at the Home Office, Sir George Chrystal at the Ministry of Health suggested that the government would find it difficult to explain why the Anderson plan remained inoperative.[33] Sir Maurice Holmes, permanent under secretary at the Board of Education, drew the lesson that evacuation planning must be taken from the Home Office and placed in the hands of the Ministry of Health and the Board of Education.[34]

The government met the criticism in two ways. First, it brought Sir John Anderson into the cabinet as Lord Privy Seal in charge of civil defense planning. This capped a startling rise for a man who had been in parliament for less than a year. But it was widely recognized as a fitting reward for his work on the committee. By bringing in an ostensibly non-partisan spokesman for civil defense, the government hoped to deflect criticism of its record. Secondly, the government removed evacuation responsibility from the Home Office and gave it jointly to the Ministry of Health and the Board of Education--an echo of Holmes' earlier suggestion. Anderson himself announced the change to the House of Commons on 14 November 1938 in one of his first official acts. The new arrangement made sense for a variety of reasons. Evacuation planning had gone far beyond the prevention of mass panic and crowd control which had been the original rationale for placing it under the Home Office. The Anderson Report had stressed the necessity of welfare services for evacuees in the reception areas, a task better suited to the Ministry of Health which would also oversee the billeting of evacuees. The Board of Education would look to the schooling of evacuee children.

The new administrative arrangement for the implementation of evacuation was placed in a division of the Ministry of Health under J.C. Wrigley, Director of Housing and Principal Assistant Secretary of the Ministry. Four senior administrative staff from the Board of Education and three from the London County Council were seconded to this unit. Policy questions would be argued out in an Advisory Committee made up of officials from the Ministry of Health, the Board of Education and representatives from the LCC, other local educational authorities, and urban and district council members. The chairman, Sir George Chrystal, reported directly to the Minister of Health. The Advisory Committee led a moderately active life, meeting twenty times in the next eighteen months.[35] It dealt with specific problems referred to it by the Ministry of Health or the Board of Education, such as the provisions of blankets and bedding for evacuees, accommodation for pregnant mothers who accompanied their children, and the co-ordination of transport. The work of the Advisory Committee was complemented by another new policy making body, the CID Civil Defense (Policy) Sub-Committee, chaired by the ubiquitous Sir John Anderson. Its first meeting, held in December, 1938, was charged with the task of reviewing the planning and organization of all departments concerned with civil defense.[36] In time, this committee seems to have displaced all others responsible for evacuation policy.

It may seem that the evacuation was in danger of being over-planned; but Anderson was determined that nothing should slip through the administrative net. After this re-organization, circulars and advice once again flowed out to the local authorities. The first task for reception area authorities was a survey of all available accommodation for the expected flood of evacuees. On the basis of the accommodation survey, reception area authorities were allotted a specific number of evacuees. In early 1939, a series of conferences between ministerial officials and local authorities took place. This proved a useful forum for exchanging views at first hand. The conference also pulled together the various administrative strands running between the central and local authorities, and allowed trouble spots to be diagnosed early. When the town clerk of Rugby, for example, predicted the 'most ghastly muddle' if evacuees were sent there, a liason officer was dispatched to soothe and advise.[37]

By the summer of 1939, the operational side of the evacuation was firmly in place. Evacuation planning--and civil defense generally--had come a considerable distance since the early days of the 1920s. From its covert origins with essentially military objectives, evacuation had gradually incorporated other goals: educational and some social planning had been recognized as important. The changes had come about as circmstances had altered and new ideas were brought forward. Sir John Anderson, Herbert Morrison, the LCC education officers, senior civil servants, and parliament had all contributed to the shaping of the new policy. Yet it must be said that the evacuation never entirely outgrew the early assumptions of its original planners.

NOTES

1. Terence H. O'Brien, Civil Defense, (London, 1955), ch. 1.

2. See Franklyn Arthur Johnson, Defense by Committee: The British Committee of Imperial Defense, 1935-1959, (London, 1960).

3. John W. Wheeler-Bennett, *John Anderson: Viscount Waverly* (London, 1962).

4. PRO HO 45/230811, 20 October 1927.

5. O'Brien, *Civil Defense*, p. 16.

6. PRO CAB 46/23, 25 March 1931.

7. PRO CAB 46/22, 13 March 1931.

8. Committee of Imperial Defense, 'Review of the Work of the Air Raid Precautions Department' (May 1936), p. 14. A copy may be found in Hodsoll papers, Churchill College, Cambridge HDSL 4/15.

9. Hodsoll Papers, HDSL 4/1 (1935).

10. Hodsoll Papers, HDSL 6/1.

11. Hansard, H of C, vol 336, 1 June 1938, col 2096.

12. PRO HO 45/18164. Anderson made these remarks to a deputation from the Association of Municipal Corporations on 10 March 1939; and to the Consultative Committee of Local Authorities of Scotland on 6 March 1939.

13. Hansard, vol 329, 15 November 1937, cols 41-165.

14. See especially chs 12-19 in Bernard Donoghue and G.W. Jones, *Herbert Morrison: Portrait of a Politician* (London, 1973).

15. Hansard, vol 329, 15 November 1937.

16. Hansard, vol 336.

17. PRO HO 45/18163.

18. Hansard, vol 336, 26 May 1938, col 1380.

19. PRO HO 45/17636, Minutes of the Anderson Committee.

20. GLRO EO/WAR/1/3, 24 May 1938. Lowndes' version of evacuation planning may be found in

Chapters XII and XIII of his _Silent Social Revolution_ (Oxford U., 1969), 2nd ed.

21. GLRO EO/WAR/1/3, meeting of 14 June 1938.

22. Report of Committee on Evacuation (London HMSO, 1938) Cmd 5837.

23. R.M. Titmuss, _Problems of Social Policy_ (London, 1976), rev ed, p. 28.

24. See Lowdnes' account in GLRO EO/WAR/1/4.

25. _Ibid_.

26. _Evening News_, 27 October 1938; _The Times_ 31 October 1938.

27. Wiltshire Record Office, Clerks 273/1 WAR

28. Gloucestershire Record Office, C/CDa V 5/2

29. Shropshire Record Office, County Council Bundle System--Evacuation 161A, Box 21.

30. Hansard, vol 340, 3 November 1938, cols 419, 429.

31. GLRO EO/WAR/1/4.

32. GLRO EO/WAR/1/7, letter to Sir Philip Game, Commissioner of Police of the Metropolis, 4 November 1938.

33. PRO HLG 68/5, 17 September 1938.

34. _Ibid_., 16 September 1938. See also Holmes' minute paper of 5 October 1938 in PRO ED 136/116.

35. The minutes will be found in PRO ED 136/110, ED 136/111, ED 136/113, and ED 136/114.

36. The minutes are in PRO MH 79/86 and PRO MH 79/87.

37. GLRO EO/WAR/1/11, letter of 7 July 1939.

CHAPTER THREE

Children in the Country

When German troops invaded Poland on 1 September 1939, the code word 'Pied Piper' set in motion the evacuation. Although there were some tears and unhappiness among the thousands of evacuees, calm and order predominated. Careful planning had no doubt contributed to the holiday mood. Active preparation had been underway since late August when schools opened for early sessions and teachers were recalled from holidays to advise parents and children. Teachers also conducted evacuation rehearsals and inspected luggage and gas masks. When the evacuation order came to London, teachers guided 600,000 scholars, mothers, and small children to 168 entraining stations for the journey to the country. Scenes similar to those in London occurred in other cities where air raids were expected. Moving out by school groups proved a great success.

During the first four days of September, trains filled with evacuees fanned out from London filling in an area south of a line from Land's End to the Wash. The distribution of evacuees roughly followed main line railway service. Schools within reach of Waterloo station found themselves in Dorset and Devon; those near Paddington were deposited all along the Great Western Railway from Berkshire to Cornwall; while St. Pancras schools were largely in Bedforshire and Marylebone schools in Buckinghamshire. The heaviest concentration of evacuees was in Sussex because of the available accommodation in resort towns such as Brighton, Hove, and Eastborne. There were also high concentrations in Bedforshire, Northamptonshire,

Hertfordshire, Kent, and Surrey. In this first evacuation, relatively few went to more distant southwestern counties.

Organization in the reception areas was equally smooth. Here the voluntarism of the government's plan received a satisfactory trial. The Boy Scouts ran messages, St. John's Ambulance crews were on hand for emergencies, and the Women's Voluntary Service arranged for the immediate care and feeding of the evacuees. Most evacuees settled into private homes within hours of arrival. Some scattered reports of hosts refusing evacuees at the door were heard, but in the main the first stage of the evacuation concluded without serious mishap. Children had been dispersed to less vulnerable areas ahead of the bombs.

In the quiet weeks that followed, the military assumption which underlay evacuation from its inception--a heavy and indiscriminate bombing of civilians--failed to materialize. The German war machine was engaged elsewhere. As the weeks dragged on the initial sympathy between hosts and evacuees faded. Conflict between evacuees and hosts grew. Arguments over trivial matters flared into open hostility. Even the simple disruption of a routine could, in time, become annoying to the settled life of a community. One may imagine the impact on a quiet village such as Winnington in Bedfordshire when two busloads of evacuees from Walthamstow arrived. With a population of less than five hundred and the most important of its institutions a Tudor church and a nineteenth century chapel, Winnington held few attractions for city children.[1] Personality clashes and religious differences, however, account for only some of the problems in the reception areas. Underlying much of the resentment were distinctively different habits of thought and behavior engendered by social prejudice and class divisions. The evacuees thought their hosts 'too posh' and withdrawn: the hosts on their part complained of 'dirty' evacuees.

The government was surprised by the furor over evacuation. It had no alternatives to offer and held to its original view that heavy bombing could begin at any time. It warned evacuees to stay in place, and urged reception area authorities to encourage compliance. Because the government was bound by its voluntarist ideas, it did not enforce evacuation. The only form of compulsion lay upon reception area hosts to receive evacuees, but even this was often interpreted loosely and enforcement was applied with varying degrees of strictness. The result was confusion about the government's real policy and a gradual erosion of participation in the evacuation scheme. The story of evacuation in its early months then is the story of billeting in the reception areas. The scope of evacuation makes it impossible to examine billeting in any systematic way on a national scale. What we present in this chapter and the following is the evacuation scheme as it worked in some selected counties serving as reception areas.

Berkshire was a typical reception area--largely rural, with a mixture of small villages and some larger boroughs. In Reading, Berkshire had a substantial county town with a university. Reading's chief industries were biscuit making, seed production, brewing and light engineering. Social and economic class groupings were similar to other provincial towns. It was to Reading that the largest influx of Berkshire evacuees came, mostly from Lambeth, Battersea, and Wandsworth. When the first evacuee train from Vauxhall arrived at 10:10 a.m. on 1 September, local officials were well prepared. Reception and billeting were under the control of the city's Education Department, the education officer acting both as reception and chief billeting officer. By combining the responsibilities for education and billeting in one official, Reading acted unusually but this administrative device proved effective in avoiding some of the billeting conflicts endemic in other communities. Reading enjoyed an enviable reputation among reception areas.[2] The Education Department also provided staff who served as station marshalls: they met the trains and escorted the evacuees onto buses which carried them to Reading's schools where they were given milk, meat, biscuits and a quarter pound chocolate bar. Local teachers and volunteers at the schools, acting as billeting officers, took the provisioned children to individual homes. A similar organizational structure cared for evacuees at Abingdon, Didcot, Faringdon, Hungerford, Maidenhead, Newbury, Wantage, and Windsor. Maidenhead station was also the detraining center for the Marlow (Bucks) evacuees.

The most important evacuation officials in Reading, as in other reception areas, were the chief billeting officers.[3] They were commonly employees of district councils--borough librarians, borough treasurers, or sanitary inspectors. They rarely had special qualifications for what later became an onerous job. In the early days of the war, these officials were voluntary. Their duties were thought temporary, to cease shortly after evacuation had been completed. As it happened, their duties increased in the months ahead and in many reception areas the chief billeting officer became a salaried position, reporting directly to the local council. They organized the reception, distribution, and billeting of evacuees. They maintained billeting forms and arranged billeting transfers. They were also responsible for keeping an accurate file on the evacuees in their areas. For audit purposes they retained the receipts of billeting money paid to rural hosts through the local post offices. All stores, blankets, and boots either donated or purchased for evacuees fell under their care. To help them in these tasks, chief billeting officers could have dozens of subordinate voluntary officers.

From the outset, however, billeting officers faced severe problems. Complaints swamped them throughout September and October of 1939. Householders bombarded them requesting relief and removal of their evacuees. From one Warwickshire parish came a strong refusal to comply with any evacuation request; it was probably typical of householders who were reluctant to alter their lives to accommodate intrusive evacuees. The householder, a farmer, rose early and worked all day on his 300 acre farm as long as there was light in the sky. 'I must have rest', he wrote, 'when I come in to meals and late evenings to gain or retain strength of an arduous life'. Farm work already constituted his 'bit to help the Nation'. In addition, his wife, afflicted with 'nerves' must not overwork or worry: 'verminous children <u>or</u> <u>loud</u> expectant mothers' would force them to hire a nurse for her health. Besides, he wrote, they had agreed to take in a clergyman and his wife from London: 'they would look after themselves with assistance, I expect, of their maid'.[4] The language of prejudice revealed in this letter soon became familiar to billeting officers.

As a check on the decision of the billeting officers, Billeting Tribunals were created. They, too, were voluntary bodies. Serving as appellate boards, the Tribunals warded off from the courts all but the most difficult cases. If the extant minutes of the Rugby Billeting Tribunal are typical, exemption from billeting duties was commonly granted for a variety of reasons.[5] Accepted householder excuses included: a member of the household in essential war work; householders who were on various odd or part-time jobs; a long term illness--in fact, any medical certificate from a doctor seems to have been approved automatically; and households which had live-in relatives. Two cases of unsuccessful appeal included one householder who claimed she could not accept an evacuee because she helped her mother manage an inn. The Tribunal ruled that her mother must hire a replacement: three months were allowed after which the daughter must accept an evacuee. In another case, an appellant insisted that she had to visit her daughter's house four times weekly for housework. When this was denied, she presented a medical certificate which stated she was suffering from an old ankle injury and could not manage the work involved in taking care of an evacuee. Such an obvious case of inconsistency made the work of the Tribunal occasionally easy.

The frequency of billeting complaints may be judged from a sample of a few Berkshire communites. The chief billeting officer at Windsor had seventy callers a day in the first weeks of evacuation. In Newbury, rebilleting averaged forty to fifty transfers weekly. Numbers were higher in neighboring Maidenhead where the billeting officer made 750 transfers in the first three months of evacuation. Billeting officers channelled some complaints administratively upward to the evacuation areas, especially to London, where streams of inquiry and criticism flooded LCC offices. From that first week in September, queues formed in the long corridors at County Hall. The telephone rang continuously and post bags bulged. The LCC hired relays of shorthand typists. They hurriedly devised short forms of correspondence. LCC officials were often too busy to keep complete records, or one supposes, to commit thoughts to memos and minutes: decisions were made on the run. Mounting pressure took a heavy toll. In early November, the LCC's Education Officer, E.M. Rich, suffered a breakdown because of overwork and was absent for two months. His retirement shortly afterward was well deserved.

The most immediate complaint reaching London and the other urban evacuation areas was the dirty or verminous condition of many of the evacuees. One West county shire, where scabies had never been known, witnessed its introduction when evacuees arrived.[6] Perhaps the worst recorded incidence was in Bridgenorth (Salop) where an estimated 70% of the evacuees were verminous. There were also cases of whooping cough, scarlet fever, ringworm and serious impetigo.[7] This was an unusually high percentage: but it must be remembered that the evacuees had come from Liverpool's most disadvantaged section along the Scotland Road. Other reception areas reported far fewer cases. At Wellington, only a few miles distant from Bridgenorth, no more than one or two percent were serious enough to segregate into separate lodgings.[8]

Verminous and unclean children were proof to some that 'vast sums' of public money had been wasted on the social services: this was the substance of a resolution to the Board of Education from the Thirsk and Malton Division Conservative Association.[9] The theme of the evacuation as an unnecessary and wasteful item of public expense went the rounds in the reception areas. Local medical officers, who had borne the brunt of inspecting the evacuees, were loud in their condemnation. The evacuation was 'a howling fiasco', as the Medical Officer of Health to Leyburn Rural District Council put it. Or, as the Medical Officer to Goole Rural Council said, it was 'an intolerable hardship'. The medical officer of the Easthampstead Rural District

Council reported that a local hotel had to be rented for evacuees with 'vicious and dirty habits'.[10]

Local council members proved themselves equal in hyperbole to medical officers. In Berkshire, the Faringdon District Council condemned evacuees with 'dirty habits' as unbilletable. The Wantage Rural Council heard of the 'terrible experiences' caused by evacuees who had been put into 'decent homes'. A councillor at the Wokingham Rural District Council believed that 'they had received London's problems in the Workingham district'.[11] Other councils followed Easthamstead's example, informing the Ministry of Health that it would not accept further evacuees unless special hostels could be established.

Of course, it was sometimes true that evacuees arrived unclean. But the dirt could be washed away: scabies and nits, too, were easily treated. The implication of householder complaints was that the so-called 'dirt diseases' of scabies, impetigo, and lousiness--and dirt itself--were somehow joined with faults of character or the imperfections of lower class habits and behavior. The association of hygiene with character was nicely drawn by the Times Educational Supplement in one of its leading articles. Criticizing evacuees' behavior, the TES wrote: 'Brushing their teeth and saying their prayers were exercises of which they knew nothing'.[12] Distinctions between decent middle class homes and slum-dwelling evacuees were more sharply made in the conservative journal, The Spectator. Shortly after the evacuation had begun, R.C.K. Ensor wrote from one of the home counties that many of the mothers 'were the lowest grade of slum women--slatternly malodorous tatterdemalions trailing children to match'.[13] His colleague, W.L. Burn, agreed. Only one third of the evacuated women were tolerable, Burn believed; the remainder thought of evacuation as 'a cheap country holiday of infinite duration'. The evacuees were increasing the burden of 'middle-class women living in chronically understaffed houses'. What good was it, Burn asked rhetorically, to have in the countryside town children 'who represent the antithesis of all that the decent patient country housewife has striven to instill into her own children?'[14]

Upper-class criticism of the evacuees seemed occasionally tinged with an amused condescension. Lady Diana Cooper (wife of Duff Cooper, who served for a short time as Minister of Information in the early days of the war) reported that her evacuees never left their lodging. 'I see their dough-coloured faces glued to the windows', she wrote. 'I suppose it's the livestock that scares the parents'.[15] She also wrote of the regrettable disruption the evacuation had caused the owners of large houses nearby. Aubussons had to give way to linoleum; antique furnishings were replaced by barrack-like beds. Heirlooms and pictures were pushed aside for cradles and nurses. In the gardens of these homes, 'exhausted and cumbersome women lay panting in last-word Fortnum and Mason garden chairs, staring at turquoise bathing-pools....They yearned for their street of neighbours and familiar surroundings, however squalid'.[16] In a patronizing attitude more alarmist in tone, F. Tennyson (Fryn) Jesse wrote to her American friends that the children in evacuee families were bound to grow up into 'sub-human savages' unless they could be saved somehow. The only law these children seemed to know was 'the law of the jungle'. They would eventually become 'a greater danger to the realm than explosive bombs'.[17] This was a sentiment shared by the wife of an RAF pilot who counted herself lucky not to have evacuees. The evacuees, she confided in a letter to a friend, 'have caused more trouble than the Germans. They come from the worst part of Liverpool and the colour varies from black to yellow'.[18] So pervasive was the anti-evacuee mood that it strained Christian mercy: The Reading and District Congregational Monthly wondered whether it was wise even in wartime to accept diseased children and whether there was 'any necessity for the spoilation of decent homes and furniture, the corruption of speech and moral standards of our own children by the irruption into their midst of those who...bring such laxity with them'.[19]

Disease and illness among the evacuees which helped fan rural outrage was real enough. The precise extent of ill-health among the evacuees is difficult to determine, but it could have been substantial in some reception areas. The most thorough examination of the problem was made by Dr. Kenneth Mallanby, Research Fellow at the University of Sheffield. He investigated the incidence of pediculosis in the reception areas at the request of the Ministry of Health and Board of Education. Collecting data from the fever hospitals in ten industrial cities, Mallanby found that practically 50% of the children under five were infested. In contrast, less than three percent of the children in rural southern counties were infested. The report was based on the records of 60,000 children. The findings were so shocking that the ministries concerned debated whether or not to publish them. If released publically, it could provide a propaganda victory for Germany. Sir Maurice Holmes at the Board of Education, however, believed that the report showed a state of affairs that was 'a disgrace' to a civilized country. Not only should it be published as a government document, but maximum publicity should attend it: otherwise, infestation might increase. The Ministry of Health opposed this idea and supported a compromise position whereby the report would be summarized and issued in a circular to public health authorities who could then make improvements.[20]

The long term effects of the vermin scare was a legacy of mistrust and misunderstanding between reception and evacuation areas. A tug of war developed in some reception areas as local authorities sought ways of expelling evacuees and evacuation authorities tried to keep them in place. This could not help but affect the morale of evacuee staff and children in questions wholly unconnected with vermin. A well-documented incident of this sort occurred in Berkshire over the disposition of an 'open air' school evacuated to Winnersh, near Reading.[21] Open air schools were special establishments for children in delicate health who had been exposed to tuberculosis. Although not infectious, they might be considered potentially so: their attendance at a special school at least implied particular care should be taken with their health. Yet when the Springwell House Open Air School at Clapham was evacuated to Winnersh, the children were dispersed among private homes. Learning that they had billeted upon them a potential tubercular child, foster parents raised an immediate outcry. Householder opinion was reflected in the Wokingham Rural District Council (in whose jurisdiction Winnersh was). The Council was wholly unsympathetic to the school. Indeed, the headmistress blamed the 'great difficulties' of the school on the 'opposition, petty persecution and general unpleasantness' of the Council's officials. She reported that the children were restless and unhappy about the episode. The regional school inspector agreed with the headmistress; he thought there was 'abundant evidence' that the Council did not intend to cooperate with the government's evacuation scheme. Even the medical officer was unsympathetic to Springwell House--so much so that the inspector believed the school should be transferred from East Berks. A series of letters was exchanged between the Wokingham Council and the LCC Education Office. Wokingham charged the LCC with carelessness. Eventually all the children were examined and found in excellent health. This did not satisfy the Council: the children could still become tubercular. They resolved to send the children back to their homes. At this point in the dispute, the Ministry of Health stepped in. Its Senior Regional Officer at Reading called a conference in late December 1939 to vent the grievances. The LCC medical officer in attendance explained that open air schools were merely precautionary establishments: no infectious case was in fact admitted. In addition, Springwell House was not residential but a day school. This at last satisfied the Council and they dropped their attempt to remove the school.

A residue of ill feeling remained. London had been partially at fault for not taking the necessary care early on to inform fully the Wokingham Council about the special nature of the school. It also appears that they were not entirely candid about Springwell House: there was one suspected case of lupus. On the other hand, the affair was also fuelled in part by hostile householders. Springwell House was in this sense only a flashpoint. On a sensitive issue demanding more than the usual amount of tact, neither side had performed particularly well. More ominous from the government's point of view was the strong evidence of householder dislike for the evacuation scheme.

Unhappily, the vermin scare was only the first in a wave of complaints against the evacuees. Foster parents reported numerous cases of enuresis. Householders burned their sheets and bed-linen and requested grants from local authorities for replacement costs. Even otherwise kindly disposed householders believed that bed-wetting was a flaw of character and discipline. In one Devon case, a householder repeatedly caned an eight year old evacuee 'because he had tried everything else to break him' of his bad habit.[22] It was not well understood in the reception areas that children from working class families were facing a significant psychological adjustment upon their removal to a new environment. Studies made within a few months of the evacuation made this clear, although the severity and extent of the adjustment is a matter of debate. Estimates ranged from 80% of all evacuees as bed-wetters immediately after evacuation to considerably smaller percentages in the weeks that followed. The numbers were high enough to add to the growing unpopular image of evacuees in the reception areas.

The chorus of complaints reaching London and other evacuation areas began to take on an official tone as local councils increasingly became the spokesmen for rural householders. The councils believed the LCC and similar evacuation officials had been negligent: more care ought to have been taken with the children's condition before evacuation. In its defense, the LCC explained that the evacuation had taken place at the end of holidays before school medical services could be brought fully into play. There simply had not been time enough to examine thoroughly every child. It was surely most important, the LCC maintained, that children be moved rapidly from vulnerable areas: health problems could then be dealt with in comparative safety. In any case, the LCC believed the councils were prone to exaggeration. The LCC claimed that only ten percent of its children were verminous when evacuated.[23] Unfamiliar with the habits and hygenic conditions of the urban poor, local councils too readily lumped together superficially undesirable characteristics. At Leicester City, for example, the Clerk of the Council complained to the Ministry of Health that fully 75% of mothers with preschoolers were objectionable on grounds of health, habits, or character. An investigation by the senior regional officer revealed that the complaint was 'completely overdrawn': only fifteen percent at most were objectionable.[24]

Unhappiness in the billets arose from circumstances other than disease and dirt. In a few cases, very young evacuees were billetted on old age pensioners who simply lacked the energy to manage lively youngsters. Even in younger households, children suddenly added could be a difficult burden. Where mothers came with children, overcrowding in the kitchens and bathrooms naturally led to friction. Petty grievances mounted. An evacuee boy spoiled a householder's garden; another ate too much. Parents visiting evacuee children expected lavish hospitality. Householders had to purchase clothing or boots for their evacuees, many of whom had arrived either in tatters, or in clothing unsuitable to the fast approaching and inevitably wet and muddy country winter. Was it fair, asked an evacuation organizer, that reception areas 'should have to <u>clothe</u> the children as well as <u>clean</u> them!'[25]

Billeting problems of a special sort arose from religious differences between evacuees and householders. There were particular problems with Roman Catholic and Jewish evacuees. Among Catholics, grievances were of two kinds. First, some Catholic schools had been sent to heavily protestant areas lacking appropriate religious facilities. It was not always easy to rectify this inconvenience to professing Catholic evacuees. Only after extensive negotiations, for example, between the Clun (Salop) Rural District Council and various other local and national officials was a settlement reached that allowed children from a Catholic working-class parish in Liverpool to attend mass. Even then, the outcome was not very satisfactory: the parish was eventually forced to pay bus fares for transportation to a neighboring community--an expense they could ill afford. The Clun authorities, in turn embarrassed and then angered by the letters from the parish, requested that only protestant evacuees be sent them in the future.[26] A second grievance among Catholics was the evidence of a strong anti-Catholic sentiment in the countryside. It was highest in the Welsh valleys to which largely Catholic Liverpool and Birmingham evacuees had been sent. The Catholic hierarchy made strong representations, asking the government to re-group Catholic schools into more sympathetic reception areas. Arthur Cardinal Hinsley, Archbishop of Westminster, appealed directly to the President of the Board of Education. The Archbishop also announced the creation of a Catholic Commission with plenary powers to arrange re-billeting. The request was taken up by officials at the Ministry of Health, who were sympathetically inclined. But re-billeting on any grounds was becoming difficult as criticism grew in reception areas. The matter was complicated by the fact that in some places Catholic evacuees and Protestant householders were perfectly satisfied with billeting arrangements. This was the case of Kensal Newtown School which had been evacuated to rural parishes around Devizes. The Ministry believed that the Catholic Commission was unnecessarily roiling the waters at Devizes. Caught in the middle between the Catholic authorities on the one hand and satisfied evacuees on the other, the Ministry eventually went the way of the Commission and relocated the school at Paignton, in the larger Torbay urban area.[27]

Jewish evacuees had similar experiences in the countryside, although their difficulties were compounded by what appeared to be unnecessarily exotic ritual. When the Jewish Secondary School from London was evacuated to Bedfordshire, there were difficulties from the first.[28] At the depot, they were given brown bags filled with corned beef, biscuits, and tinned milk--none of it kosher. Some evacuees were greeted by their foster parents with inviting ham omelettes. The day after their arrival, a Saturday, several of the scholars were asked to run errands. Polite refusals on the grounds of the Jewish Sabbath were not easily accepted. The local vicar, too, was disappointed: he had hoped to fill his Sunday

School choir with new recuits. During the Sukkoth holiday, some of the children went to a nearby wood and cut branches to construct the traditional _sukkah_ or hut, to remind them of the days of wandering of the ancient Jewish tribes. The owners of the woods were not pleased. In some cases, of course, Jewish customs once explained were accepted. But not always. As the Clerk of the Bedfordshire County Council put it to his Director of Education, the Jewish evacuees 'presented many problems' and there was 'no doubt that many of the villagers [were] getting very restive and discontented'.[29]

Jewish evacuees had perhaps most difficulty in maintaining their dietary codes. To safeguard these, London's Chief Rabbi appointed a Kosher Canteen Committee. It met initial success in establishing kosher canteens for concentrations of Jewish evacuees in Bishop's Stortford and St. Ives (Hunts). Elsewhere the Canteen Committee faced difficulty. Local education authorities were reluctant to increase administrative burdens in hard pressed reception areas, especially where the numbers of Jewish evacuees were very small. Conflict developed between the authorities at King's Lynn and the Canteen Committee over the precise number of Jewish evacuees in and around that borough: the Committee claimed that there were 220; the authorities (without citing a number) claimed this was too large. The controversy was referred to the Board of Education, one of whose inspectors enquired discreetly into the matter. The inspector upheld the King's Lynn authorities' estimate and the Canteen Committee was so informed. Nudged by the Committee, the Board took further action, enquiring of local educational authorities around the country what provisions had been made for Jewish evacuees. The Board eventually recommended separate Kosher kitchens in communities with more than one hundred Jewish evacuees. The Canteen Committee would reimburse the authority for any added costs incurred. How willingly local authorities complied with the Board's recommendation is unclear, although the Canteen Committee had an active life into the middle years of the war.[30]

Perhaps nothing alarmed rural householders

more about the evacuation than the growth of juvenile crime in the reception areas. To rural householders, the cause was obvious: the countryside had been flooded with rough children and hooligans from the cities. Local newspapers published detailed accounts of evacuees brought before magistrates. A leading article in the _North Berks Herald_ expressed a common belief when it observed that 'a considerable proportion' of young offenders in the recent upswing in crime were London evacuees.[31] Certain instances lent credence to this belief. On a single day, eleven pupils from Chelsea were charged at Chertsey (Surrey) Juvenile Court for petty larceny.[32] The Northampton court heard nineteen cases involving London evacuees in October, 1939.[33] Fifty London evacuees appeared before Worthing magistrates in the first four months of evacuation.[34] From March 1940 to March 1941, London children were involved in 806 cases of larceny in the reception areas.[35] Kettering officials described some London evacuees as 'thorough little toughs, most destructive': two brothers, aged ten and eleven, were caught thieving four times within a matter of days. One seven year old had a hysterical temper and a sharp Bowie knife which he repeatedly drew out before being forcibly disarmed.[36]

There is little doubt that juvenile delinquency increased in the first years of the war. Family dislocation and wartime disorientation may have been contributing factors. Perhaps the evacuation itself was at fault. Joyce Carey's _Charley is My Darling_ sets out convincingly in fictional form the adventures of a London evacuee who must prove himself to his country companions: he is eventually led to a career of crime in the West Country. Official statistics seem to confirm reception area impressions and fictional accounts. Indictable offenses for adolescents thirteen years of age and under increased 41% from 1938-39 to 1939-40. The increase among adolsecents fourteen to seventeen was 22%.[37]

But this was not the whole of the story. Home Office statistics were for the entire country, not merely the reception areas. More importantly, it was a trend begun before the war.

From the mid-1930's there had been a perceptible rise in the number of offenses among the young. Police constables were convinced of a genuine increase in crime. The Home Office, however, thought it was due very likely to a statistical artifact. When the Children and Young Persons Act of 1933 increased the age at which a young person could be charged as a juvenile from sixteen to seventeen, larger numbers came before the juvenile courts.[38]

In short, there is no conclusive proof that evacuees were a significant factor in reception area criminal statistics. Yet they were often perceived to be. What lay behind this perception? More broadly speaking, what lay behind the unfavorable perception of all evacuees among so many rural hosts? The answer must be complex. As we have indicated in our examples above, reasons range from personal to religious. Perhaps anti-Semitism was at work against Jewish evacuees, especially after the Kosher Canteen Committee became active in the reception areas. Anti-Catholic sentiment, historically strong in Britain, was surely a factor in the more provincial and protestant areas of the country. And one cannot discount the natural revulsion among tidy countrymen at the sight of filthy and infested urban slum children at their doors. Yet so immediate was the outcry in some areas and so sustained was it that there seems to have been a predisposition to dislike the evacuees. They were perceived as a threat, rather than unfortunate displaced wartime refugees. As the incidents of householder disaffection mounted, they gradually formed a pattern.

It seems clear that to the suspicious householders the evacuees represented the dangerous working classes of urban Britain. Country hosts thus thought of the evacuees in stereotypical terms. A well documented example occurred in Chatteris, Cambridgeshire. Chatteris was then a town of about 5000 set in a prosperous farming district. When evacuees arrived, they were described among townsmen as '"typical" East Enders'--that is, conforming to stereotypes. The women had two or more children; some were expectant mothers. Many of the women were 'painted and powdered' and some lit cigarettes as soon as they got off the buses, 'unusual sights amongst the middle-class, chapel-going folk of Chatteris', as a Mass Observation reporter noted. The children were untidy. All looked pathetic as they shambled into the makeshift evacuation center.[39] There were similar scenes elsewhere. At Great Missenden (Bucks.), evacuees were said to stand about looking not only dirty but discontented as well.[40] In one small Cheshire village, hosting several 'Irish slum women' from Liverpool, local matrons were said to be indignant that their picturesque black and white village was spoiled by 'those women in shawls'.[41]

Not every negative reaction to the evacuees invited simple rejection. Some rural hosts wanted to reform their evacuees. In one Devon farmhouse, two ladies from Sidbury were in charge of twenty mothers and thirty children. The ladies were astonished by the child rearing methods of the evacuee mothers. As they told a neutral observer: 'If the mothers want the children to behave, they hit them'. This could not be allowed to continue. 'We must give the children training' they concluded.[42] One evacuation organizer, writing from Lincolnshire, suggested that mothers be excluded entirely from the billeting scheme because so many of them were of the 'low, slum type'. Children of such mothers should be put into nursery schools and cared for properly, their mothers to be banished to camps or hostels where they could 'live dirtily (and happily) together and be a nuisance to no one but themselves.[43]

So extensive a disenchantment with evacuation in provincial areas naturally engaged the attention of the national press. One of the earliest investigative accounts was by H. de Winton Wigley of the liberal News Chronicle. Wigley toured reception areas in Buckinghamshire and Berkshire in October, 1939.[44] At first, his articles painted a rosy picture of the evacuation. By his fourth article, Winton's ideas had undergone a change: 'when I began this tour', he wrote, 'I was not prepared to hear of conditions that have made women voluntary helpers weep, have upset scores of homes and brought some housewives to a state of nervous prostration'. Householders were not prepared, continued Winton, 'to receive into their decent homes filthy children whose personal hygiene "are worse than those of some domestic animals" in the words of more than one billeting official'. Wigley cited as sources two prominent Berkshire women--one a village billeting officer, another a rural district council and parish councillor. Both told Wigley that evacuees should be in camps, rather than in the private homes 'of clean, healthy families'. They, too, wondered aloud if the millions 'spent on much-boosted social service in London should not produce better results than these'. Wigley's final article firmly took the side of householders against the evacuees: 'the number of misfits is so great that it was necessary to call it to the attention of the public at large'.

As Wigley's article suggests, there were few attempts to scrutinize evacuation from the evacuee point of view. Indeed, it is difficult to find direct evidence of evacuee opinions. Evacuees could not easily voice their frustrations and had little opportunity to make public their grievances. In contrast to reception area residents, who looked upon their county newspapers as friendly forums, evacuees rarely wrote letters to the editors. In any case, most of the evacuees were children which precluded any extensive written record. Only a few older students kept diaries. In short, evacuee attitudes must be largely determined from sources other than the evacuees themselves. Evacuee teachers were a useful source (as we shall see in Chapter IV). Reception area residents, sympathetic to the plight of the evacuees, were also helpful. But these must be used with caution because they often seem grounded in a left-wing or progressive point of view. This is especially true of material found in the Mass Observation Survey at the University of Sussex. Three of Mass Observation's most informative diaries have obvious sympathies with the Labor Party: one was a member of the Left Book Club; another an avid reader of the New Statesman; and a third strongly opposed right-wing habits of thought.[45] People of progressive views were probably more acutely aware of the shortcomings of a conservative government and its failures in social policy.

Yet biased opinions need not be cast out of court. If what is said can be substantiated by other evidence, we may use them with confidence. Even divergent evacuation experiences can provide useful information when examined carefully. This is clearly illustrated by the following two examples. In the first, a schoolgirl of seventeen was evacuated from London to a small, semi-industrial town identified as 'L' thirty miles from London. Half her schoolmates--'well brought up middle class girls and boys', as she put it--were placed 'in tiny, dirty houses' where the girls were treated as 'unpaid maids'.[46] This evacuee's (atypical) middle class social origins are obvious. In contrast was the experience of another London school girl evacuated to a rectory at Deal. 'The house and food were all right', she wrote, 'but the people were snobbish blue-blooded Tories'.[47] When we learn that she was a member of the Young Communist League, her comments can be placed in perspective. As different as their social and political attitudes may have been, the two girls agreed on one point--the attitude of what were termed the 'well-to-do' of the reception areas. The middle-class girl who had gone to 'L'. remarked, almost wistfully, on the number of 'clean, middle class homes' in the city; but she also observed that 'the owners of these homes have seen to it that they did not have to take in evacuees'.[48] The young communist wrote in like manner of her foster home: 'The rectory is the biggest house in Deal, yet they took in four children. There were seven large rooms in the house which were not used'.[49]

These observations of two London school girls brings into sharp relief perhaps the most significant aspect of the evacuation story, and allows us to make a more precise distinction between those reception area residents who accepted evacuees and those who rejected them. Generally speaking, it seems that wealthy and middle class householders avoided evacuation duty. Working class inhabitants of the reception areas welcomed the evacuees--or at least tolerated them in a benign fashion. A typical example occurred in Chatteris. A billeting officer there (who was also a Mass Observation reporter) visited several wealthy residents whose large houses had been assigned three or more evacuees. At each of these he wrote, 'we were met with refusals and rudeness--they 'weren't going to have such women or kids in their places'.[50] Not until 9:30 in the evening were the evacuees settled, and then mainly in the small houses of poorer residents, many of whom took in two, three, or four evacuees when scheduled for only one. The generosity of the poorer cottagers occasionally went to considerable lengths. One elderly crippled bachelor gave up his only bedroom and made a shakedown in his workshop so that he could take more evacuees than he had been assigned. Other billeting officers at Chatteris reported 'exactly the same difficulties': they, too, were greeted 'with various excuses, complaints, and abuse'. Only one billeting officer met with success: his district comprised the newly built Council Housing Estate occupied entirely by working-class families.

Evidence from other reception areas substantiate the events at Chatteris. In Macclesfield, Cheshire, one young teacher, who conducted a survey for evacuee accommodation, discovered that on the whole 'the poorer people were kinder, friendlier, and far more anxious to pull their weight'. She found one woman, a piece worker in a factory, who asked for time off to receive her allotted evacuees.[51] 'We find over and over again', wrote a WVS regional administrator, 'that it is the really poor people who are willing to take evacuees and that the sort of bridge playing set who live at such places as Chorley Wood are terribly difficult about it all'.[52]

Reception area hostility among the 'well-to-do' increased as Christmas 1939 drew near. A senior regional officer in the Ministry of Health predicted 'a riot' from the affluent if their homes were not free for relatives and friends.[53] In Durham, some householders shut their homes for the holidays and moved away temporarily, forcing out their evacuees. Or, more deviously, they feigned illness and sent their evacuees home; once gone, the evacuees were asked not to return.[54] Thus, fifty girls from King Edward's High School in Birmingham lost their billets over the holidays.[55] In Cumberland, officials of the Cockermouth Urban District Council who attempted to find billets for Tyneside evacuees returning after Christmas were rebuffed. The problem was eventually solved when a youth hostel was placed at their disposal.

The resistance of Cockermouth residents found a sympathetic response, however. As one letter to the Yorkshire Post put it: 'it is time that the 'Cockermouth' spirit was shown in all districts'.[56] Householder truculence became blatant enough by late 1939 that it forced some district and local councils into action. Shortly after Christmas, the Richmond [Yorks] Town Council took steps to ensure an equitable distribution of evacuees in the town after a Councillor reported that poorer citizens 'were complaining that there were many people in better circumstances and with better facilities who had never had any children billeted with them since the start of the scheme'.[57] But other district councils supported wealthy householders' actions. In Berkshire the Easthampton Rural District Council ruled that evacuees who went home for Christmas and did not return by 6 January forfeited their billets.[58] At Bracknell, within Easthampton's jurisdiction, only one well-to-do householder kept his evacuees after Christmas.[59] Bracknell, in fact, seems to have been an evacuation black spot--'almost hopeless' in the opinion of the regional school inspector.[60] The Council and the inhabitants had been 'deliberately obstructive' in billeting the Brixton School of Building, a junior technical school. No less an authority than E.G. Savage, education officer of the LCC, agreed. The Brixton School had gotten 'a raw deal...at the hands of the well-to-do population in Bracknell, and I am afraid', Savage wrote to the inspector, that 'instances of this kind were going to rankle a very long time in the minds of those who have suffered'.[61]

The geography of evacuation and the pattern of discrimination against the evacuees as it developed by late 1939 is well illustrated at Wantage, the center of a small reception area in Berkshire. Wantage and eleven nearby villages lie in the Vale of the White Horse at the foot of the Berkshire downs. In the heart of a rich agricultural district, it is the sort of picturesque country described by guide books as having 'sheltered combes' and 'clear, chalk streams' with numerous half-timbered and thatched cottages. At the beginning of the war, the population of Wantage was 3400. The outlying villages had populations from two to six hundred: all were farming communities. The Chief Billeting Officer at Wantage was an official of the Berks County Council. Billeting officers in the villages under his direction included local gentry, clergymen, farmers and their wives, and an occasional teacher. A Billeting Tribunal set up to adjudicate billeting problems was made up of a priest, the chairman of the Council, the Chief Billeting Officer, and a woman councillor active in social work. The scale of billeting problems may be judged by the fact that at first the Tribunal met daily, later tapering off to twice-weekly meetings. As finally settled, more than one third of the evacuated children in Wantage town were evacuated to the three council housing estates. Another third were in the outlying working class areas. Belmont and the Charlton Road district, both of which were Victorian villa developments, had only eleven children. The larger houses around the market square and the church had an even smaller number: only a minority of their owners were willing to receive evacuees. Many larger households apparently took it for granted that evacuees would be sent to the smaller houses because the weekly allowances for evacuees 'were of value to the working class but not worth consideration by them'. One or two wealthy householders had filled their homes with relatives and thus claimed they had no available accommodation.[62] Titmuss among others believed that like unto like in the reception areas would contribute in the long run to a successful evacuation.[63] But this approach to billeting could also serve as a justification, as in Wantage, for the wealthy to avoid evacuation duties.

It may be argued that the failure of the evacuation during the autumn of 1939 and the winter of 1939-40 can be attributed to the unexpected course of the war. The anticipated heavy bombings had not materialized; in fact, there was scarcely any bombing at all. The so-called 'phoney war' diminished the appeal to patriotism that the government had hoped would motivate rural householders to accept evacuees.

Once the bombs fell in earnest, the government believed that the country would rise to the occasion and accept evacuees. Rich and poor alike would pull together in finding homes for the evacuees. Throughout the spring and early summer of 1940, there was little to test this theory. By September, however, the blitz of London was at last underway. How did this turn of events affect the reception areas?

We cannot be precise as to the numbers involved, but there is a fair certainty that reception area hosts were no more willing to accept evacuees in September 1940 than they had been a year earlier. In fact, attitudes may have hardened as the raids reversed the flow of drift back and pushed large numbers of evacuees once again into the countryside. Even before the heaviest bombing had begun, local authorities faced severe difficulty in revising their billeting lists. Of thirty-one wealthy homes in Hungerford asked to receive their share of new evacuees in the summer of 1940, only one consented. Several householders excused themselves on the grounds that if they accepted evacuees, their servants would give notice.[64] A similar reason for refusing evacuees was advanced by a rural district council in Wiltshire when it wrote to the Ministry of Health that large houses in their district could not be utilized because 'the servant problem is acute and it would be unfair to billet children in them'.[65] Reports from around the country substantiate these tales of resistant householders. A Welsh miner noticed that 'whilst the small houses are being loaded to overcrowding the private mansions are still only occupied by caretakers'. From Burford, Oxfordshire, it was reported that billeting officers were exercising their authority 'more rigorously on poor people than on rich'. Consequently, there was feeling 'that the bigger houses aren't doing their fair share'. A billeting officer in Basingstoke admitted there was difficulty persuading people to give up part of their big houses to evacuees. From Salisbury came the complaint: 'It's always the same, the poor helping the poor. There's overcrowding in every small house, and the rich still go their comfortable ways'. In Egham, Surrey, where there was open hostility to evacuees, it was reported that 'snobbery and racial feelings played quite a big part in forming this attitude'.[66]

Not every reception area had class-based complaints. A billeting officer claimed in Bagshot the 'better sort of people' had come forward, citing the Duke of Connaught who had 'taken a lot in' and Lady Ellenborough who had eight or nine evacuees.[67] And it is certainly true, as in 1939, that class distinctions between householder and evacuee cannot always account for billeting difficulties. A Catford (London) couple found themselves the victims of a Cornish woman who housed their son. She clearly sought to manipulate events to encourage his removal from her billet. She gave bad reports of the boy's behavior--once sending along a pair of trousers to be mended by the parents: the tear had come about from a dog's bite. 'I told him not to go out that way, but of course he must, and got a bite in the leg'. When character assassination failed, the householder turned to recent bombing attacks nearby. She once wrote that a 'heavy number' of people were killed (she lived near Gunnislake). In one letter, she asked to be excused from her handwriting because she was 'all of a shake' from a time bomb. She concluded with a dark hint: many of the evacuees on her road had returned home. The hint was taken, and the boy returned to Catford.[68] These examples, however, seem to represent the exceptions. The heart of the billeting controversy remained rooted in class divisions.

Reception areas' opinion on evacuation as it stood in late 1940 is usefully summed up in a survey conducted by the National Federation of Women's Institutes.[69] There were 5700 Women's Institutes in the smaller villages of England and Wales with a total membership of more than 330,000. Because WI members lived primarily in what became reception areas, most of the membership was involved in some way with the evacuation: many served as billeting officers. The object of the survey was to provide information about the conditions of the evacuees received by WI members in the summer and early autumn of 1940. The results of the survey are a distinct echo of the first evacuation a year earlier. Some evacuees and foster parents were well matched, of course, and as the report makes clear, many children were welcomed. But the general tenor of the survey was one of dismay. The survey reported the evacuation was 'a real shock' to Institute members. Careful domestic planners themselves, WI members were appalled at the apparent inability of evacuee mothers to manage a home. Although some mothers were described as capable and conscientious, 'a distressing proportion were feckless and ignorant'. Mothers seemed to fall into two types, as the survey described them: '(a) the frankly dirty and shiftless mother, (b) the mother who though passably clean or even smart herself yet seemed too indolent, bored or incompetent to train her children or look after her home'. The pamphlet published specific examples from the Institutes around the country to illustrate these generalizations. Mothers from Birmingham were condemned for their 'apathy' because they showed no inclination to knit, sew, or cook. Many of the mothers from Willesden 'lacked the will or knowledge to train their children in good habits'. Of twelve mothers from St. John and Adys Road, East Dulwich, only two 'ever did any darning or needlework'. Children from Vernon Square, King's Cross, 'were only accustomed to obey when cuffed or shouted at--this was true of at least 50 percent'. One local Institute questionnaire concluded: 'After this experience I think England ought to be proud of her country women for their cleanliness, good housewifery and decent standards'.

Antipathy to evacuees elsewhere reached extremes. In contrast to the occasional note of sympathy in the WI Survey, a die-hard opposition to evacuation had formed at Eton, Windsor, and the surrounding rural district in Berkshire. Mass Observation reported 'a very unpleasant attitude against evacuees' in Windsor: 'Hardly anyone has a good word for them'. Anti-Semitism was also marked among the householders. The evacuees, in turn, expressed 'disgust and hatred' of Windsor residents.[70] Feelings ran so high that a public debate was sparked on the evacuee question. In a lead article, the *Windsor Express* declared that 'undesirable evacuees' was one of the most difficult problems the war had produced and argued that if the law compelled people to receive strangers into their homes--strangers who may be 'ill-mannered, careless, or of unclean habits'--then the law ought also to compel them to act 'within the bounds of common decency'. Realizing the difficulty of enforcing such legislation, the Express suggested a hostel for evacuees where they could be supervised. The following week, a letter to the editor (commended by the Express to its readers), took the idea of evacuee segregation a step further. Noting that many evacuees had come from the slums and lacked even 'elementary ideas of how to behave', the writer recommended age and sexual separation for evacuee children combined with strict discipline. Adult evacuees should be treated differently. If, after every opportunity had been given for 'a proper life' and they failed to respond, they should be placed in large camps. There, isolated from others, they could manage themselves as they wished. In short, the writer concluded, 'we must use the principle of concentration camps'.[71]

No local authority carried out the threat of mass evacuee segregation, although it was certainly a topic of discussion in more than one council meeting. Most councils attempted to deal with the problem on the one hand by separating or sending back the worst evacuee offenders, and on the other by exercising a genteel show of force against the most reluctant householders. For example, in Windsor borough, a particularly difficult spot for evacuees as we have seen, policemen accompanied billeting officers on their rounds.[72] This tactic had also been considered by the borough of Bedford after billets dried up in the better parts of town.[73] Some councils brought the worst offenders before magistrates' courts. Berkshire cases consistently reveal the defendants as substantial members of the community. One householder described as a man 'of standing and education', who owned an eleven room house in a good residential neighbourhood in Maidenhead was charged at the borough session in October 1940 for refusing evacuees. 'No power on earth can make me have them', he was quoted as saying. The following month before the same court a woman described as the owner of a spacious (seven room) house was similarly charged. She had once thrown out the billeting officer, calling her 'a low, ill-bred creature'. In Wokingham, the county police court charged a resident of Finchampstead for refusing a mother and two children. The defendant claimed that her house--including three reception rooms and four bedrooms--was filled with valuable china. Besides, she had heard that evacuees were 'undesirable'. A Reading dentist and his mother were brought before the borough police court for removing evacuees from their four bedroom home in Caversham. The dentist testified that the children 'were a perfect nuisance'. Worse, he and his mother had caught flu from them. At Wantage, a member of the civil service, after a threatened compulsory billeting order, relented; but he then made the two women and three children in his care as uncomfortable as possible. He forced the use of an earthen toilet sixty yards from the house; refused them access to his kitchen; and granted them only one quart of water daily for all purposes.[74]

It would appear that councils and courts were beginning to deal effectively with householder resistance. But this would not be strictly accurate. The truth is that local authorities found themselves caught between a government intent on its policy and strong citizen opposition to it. When the authorities acted, they rarely acted firmly enough to bring about a change in householders' behavior.[75] Fines and punishment were nominal. In the examples cited above, the Maidenhead man's case was thrown out of court because of a faculty summons; the Maidenhead woman was fined three pounds. The Finchampstead resident and the Reading dentist were each fined one pound. The Wantage civil servant was fined the heaviest at ten pounds, presumably because his actions bordered on the inhumane. This somewhat feeble response on the part of the authorities should not be surprising. Each particular link in the chain of command - from magistrate to billeting officer - was forged by customary expectations. Magistrates, themselves usually householders, were naturally sympathetic to the defendants. Rural councillors would not wish to endanger their office by opposing the wishes of an influential body of householders. A borough librarian, say, serving as a billeting officer could resist only with difficulty the wishes of a leading community patron.

Undue influence was also exerted in the higher reaches of county government. In a private and confidential postscript to an official letter to a friend, the Clerk of the County Council of Bedfordshire wrote: 'I am having a Herculean task to save your house being filled with Evacuees'.[76] That local authorities sometimes seemed in collusion with upper class evasion exacerbated the sense of unfairness among evacuees and those community members who were acting responsibly. There is even some evidence that members of parliament intervened to spare their constituents the rigors of evacuation. Reports circulated in Saffron Walden (Essex) that R.A. Butler had helped some of his Tory electors avoid evacuation duties. Butler, at the time President of the Board of Education, denied the rumors. But he confided to his parliamentary secretary that his predecessor at the Board had used his influence: 'There were letters at the Board proving this', according to Butler. Nevertheless, Butler admitted the rumors were 'doing him harm'.[77]

In the evacuations that took place in the later years of the war, tensions between evacuees and hosts continued. As in 1939 and 1940, the evacuees were somtimes at fault. Indeed, it seems that evacuees had become more brazen with time. Mothers and children from the same tenement in Battersea evacuated in 1944 to Lytham St. Anne's near Blackpool demanded billets on the sea front. This they were denied; instead the billeting officer gave them return fares to London.[78] Rumor went the round in the reception areas that evacuees had adopted the slogan: 'Be evacuated and see England'. Known as 'twicers', they came to reception areas at government expense whenever they wanted a holiday. Or, in some cases, children would be sent out so that mothers could work. The government was convinced that 'twicers' were nomadic sightseers. To counter the tendency for multiple evacuation, the government introduced what it called 'selective evacuation' in late 1941. It required that an evacuee, having returned home, must show cause before re-evacuating. The criteria for showing cause and its interpretation could, however, lead to further conflict between reception areas and the cities. The town clerk of Kettering complained to the LCC in July 1942 that of 280 newly arrived evacuees, ninety-eight had been twice evacuated, seventy-two had been three times evacuated, and fifteen of them four times. The LCC apologized profusely, after which it instituted an inquiry. Results of the inquiry revealed that Kettering had considerably overstated its case: they in turn apologized. Such surface civility scarcely masked the edge of mistrust that marked their correspondence.[79]

If evacuees were occasionally at fault, evidence continues to suggest that after 1940 evacuation broke down--as in the early months of the war--because rural hosts were often unwilling to accommodate evacuees. During the spring and summer of 1941, when a rash of unhappy billeting experiences were noted in the provincial and national press, the Times Educational Supplement blamed evacuees and their parents. This point of view brought a flood of letters in rebuttal to the correspondence columns of the TES. An evacuated teacher in Wallasey, Cheshire, reported that billets were almost impossible to find because the evacuation was 'bitterly unpopular' in her region. The chair of the London branch of the Headmistresses' Association seconded this opinion: she believed that if more reception area hosts were willing to keep their evacuees, far fewer children would return to the danger zones. A teacher at the Sheffield High School wrote that, contrary to what the TES may think, evacuees were willing to stay in pleasant billets. These were mostly in the small houses: larger houses 'well known to have plenty of room consistently refuse to help'. Until the well-to-do could 'be induced to take their responsibility seriously and to accept the billeting of children of all kinds as a war-time duty and an essential form of national service', parents could not be expected to participate wholeheartedly in the evacuation program. The Headmaster of the County High School, Chingford, agreed. The early disillusionment among parents of the first evacuation had, he believed, discouraged them from continuing in the program. All of this seems to have had some effect: the TES reversed its opinion and argued that a change had to come about in the government's policy, especially the basis on which it rested--voluntary billeting.[80]

Even in the trying final year of the war, hostility against evacuees could be found in some reception areas. The flying bomb attacks during the summer of 1944 drove evacuees once again into the countryside. Billeting incidents mounted proportionately. As before, there were genuine cases of anti-social and difficult evacuees. And, as before, there were obvious cases of simple incompatibility. In Bedfordshire, a high-spirited adolescent was described by her host, a local vicar, as 'man-obsessed and sex-obsessed', behavior brought out by the arrival of American soldiers in the neighborhood. After discovering a particularly torrid letter from an American admirer, the vicar wrote the girl's parents that the soldier 'may be quite a decent fellow but my experience is that many American soldiers are very crude and ruthless in their dealing with young women'.[81] The girl was taken home soon afterward.

More relevant to our argument here were the continuing incidents, even this late in the war, of class-engendered hostility. Once again, Berkshire seemed typical. At an Easthampstead Rural District Council meeting in July 1944, the opinion was voiced that 'the higher-class householders were not playing their part in the arrangements'. Several examples were cited.[82] Two Newbury residents made the same charge, recommending that billeting officers be granted more authority to ease the shortage of accommodations.[83] A resident from Wallingford reported large houses nearby were laggard in helping the evacuees. Cottagers were asking: 'why is it that many of the 'big houses' are free from sharing this responsibility?'[84] The story was similar farther north. At Whitley Bay, 322 mothers and children spent the night at a rest center until billets could be found. In Blackpool, the civil defense controller reported an increasing number of householders raised 'unreasonable objections' to evacuees. Comparable difficulties were reported at Kettering and Scarborough. Throughout Durham and Northumberland there were billeting problems. Officials in Hoole and the surrounding area, near Chester, made strenuous efforts to billet 400 Willesden children recently arrived.[85] At Torquay, hardly any voluntary billeting was offered for the 550 mothers and children who arrived in mid-July. In Paignton, 500 mothers and children were placed in four rest centers until billeting could be settled. When a party of one hundred mothers and children arrived from London's East End, the Truro Borough council was forced to assume compulsory billeting powers, and hired two assistant billeting officers to enforce the directive.[86]

In the face of strong and persistent opposition to evacuation throughout the war, how could the program continue? There are four answers to the question. First, the government was convinced that evacuation would work and did not swerve from its commitment to the program. In practice, this policy was somewhat weakened by the government's voluntarism and by its hesitant and overly cautious approach to the most obvious cases of social prejudice. This is a topic taken up in more detail in Chapter V. A second influence working for a successful evacuation were the evacuated teachers who were responsible for their displaced young scholars. They were as committed as the government in making the scheme work. Their contribution will be discussed in Chapter IV. Third were the local authorities and leaders of opinion in the urban evacuation areas. Quite naturally, they hoped their school children would remain in the country. Mayors, councillors, members of parliament, and other evacuation officials toured reception areas persuading the evacuees to stay in place. Their efforts were supported by the urban community newspapers. In London, for example, the pages of the *East London Advertiser* and the *East End News* were filled with gratifying stories of happy evacuees. East End editors sought to reassure parents that all was well. Seldom did these papers criticize the evacuation scheme--in strong contrast to many reception area newspapers. London papers carried optimistic articles with captions such as 'Poplar Kiddies in Aylesbury' or 'Raine's School Among the Pines'. The East London press--at the risk of romanticizing evacuation--was determined to make the scheme work. A typical news article reported the Queen Mary Day Nursery of Bow housed in a twelfth century priory in Bedfordshire. King James I had once slept where now the Queen Mary's staff had their bedrooms. Some of the children were in a room with 'a genuine Gainsborough' on the wall.[87] Another story reported that the infants of the Old Church Road Nursery School in Stepney were billeted in the ancestral home of a 'well-known' peer in West Suffolk. It was 'a fairy story'.[88] Less grand, perhaps, but with the advantage of sea air were the billets of the Nicholas Gibson School, Ratcliff: they were in residences along the upper Dyke Road in Brighton. Some of the children were in homes 'with a maid, bathroom, telephone, even garage and car'.[89]

A final influence working for a successful evacuation was the good will among an unknown number of householders in the reception areas. Their quiet and kindly acceptance of evacuees was vital to the success of the program. Most of these, to be sure, were in the poorer sections of county towns and rural villages. Yet it is also true that some of the 'well-to-do' helped smooth the way, sponsoring country fairs, whist drives, and jumble sales to benefit needy evacuees. They established social clubs where evacuee mothers could go for tea and talks. The Women's Institutes managed Mothers' Clubs in the villages. At Christmas time, parties and pantomimes were arranged for evacuee children. These traditional philanthropic works were complemented by other acts of kindness. The mayor of Reading, who owned a restaurant, opened part of it rent-free to evacuees, charging pre-war prices for refreshments. For a time, one of the Reading newspapers published a regular column, 'A Corner for Evacuees'.

Perhaps the most notable of the organizations aiding the evacuees was the Women's Voluntary Service. The WVS had been specifically organized by the Home Office in 1938 to assist in ARP work. National WVS organizers emphasized that their branches must not follow their own points of view, but 'carry out the policy of the Government with regard to A.R.P., Evacuation and other services', as the Shropshire Branch was told in June 1939.[90] Headed by the Dowager Marchioness of Reading, the WVS peformed valuable services during the war, earning a well-deserved reputation for enthusiasm and reliability.[91] They were especially active in charitable causes relating to the evacuation scheme. In Abingdon alone, they collected no less than 1000 garments for necessitous children. Through their contacts in the countryside at large, they were instrumental in finding large houses suitable for children under five, a category of evacuee needing special attention.

For all their contributions to the war effort, it should not surprise us that this essentially middle and upper class organization could not discard the attitudes of a lifetime when confronted with the sudden and serious needs of an unfamiliar class.[92] The actions of the WVS were often characterized by a noticeable condescension. During an evacuation rehearsal in June 1939, the WVS sent a fleet of cars (including a Rolls Royce) fetching forty children from Islington to tea in Hertfordshire. At the end of the day, they motored the children serenely back to their homes.[93]

Once evacuation was underway, uniformed and officious WVS members occasionally riled the evacuees. WVS leadership set the tone. Lady Reading once testified before an incredulous Sir John Anderson that evacuees would be quite happy living in barns or garages in the countryside, especially if they were 'next door to a middle class house'.[94] Evacuation experiences brought a sharpened sensibility, however. Interviewed by Mass Observation in February 1940, Lady Reading admitted at last that the evacuation had been 'a most terrible fiasco'. She was especially critical of billeting facilities: 'not nearly enough use was made of the big houses of England', she told her interviewer. 'They did press the cottagers. But taken as a whole the very big houses have been the limit'.[95]

NOTES

1. Winnington Women's Institute, _Winnington_: _The History of a Bedfordshire Village_ (n.p., 1946).

2. GLRO EO/WAR/4/3, 26 April 1940.

3. A critical review of billeting officers during the war may be found in Richard Padley and

Margaret Cole (eds.), *Evacuation Survey: A Report to the Fabian Society* (London, 1940), ch. 24.

4. Warwickshire Record Office, CR 1560/65.

5. Warwickshire Record Office, CR 1557/152.

6. *Medical Officers of School Association, Annual Proceedings and Report*, No. 14 (1939-43), April 1941, Annual General Meeting.

7. PRO HLG 7/82, 16 September 1939.

8. PRO HLG 7/76, 6 September 1939.

9. PRO ED 50/196, 2 November 1939.

10. For these examples, see *Yorkshire Post*, 21 October 1939; 26 October 1939; *North Berks Herald*, 22 September 1939.

11. See *Faringdon Advertiser*, 8 September 1939; *Reading Mercury*, 9 September 1939, and 30 September 1939.

12. *TES*, 16 September 1939, in a lead article.

13. *The Spectator*, 8 September 1939.

14. *Ibid*., 22 September 1939.

15. Diana Cooper, *Trumpets from the Steep* (London, 1960), p. 85.

16. *Ibid*., p. 37.

17. F. Tennyson Jesse and H.M. Harwood, *Letters Written to America (August 1939-July 1940)*, (London, 1940), pp. 28-30.

18. Diana Forbes-Robertson and Roger W. Straus, Jr. (eds.), *War Letters from Britain*, (New York, 1941), p. 115.

19. Excerpted in the *Reading Standard*, 6 October 1939.

20. PRO ED 50/196. See also Titmuss' discussion in *Problems of Social Policy*,

pp. 125-31. Mellanby eventually published his findings in *Medical Officer*, vol. LXV (1941).

21. GLRO EO/WAR 2/29 is the general file on the incident. Other information may be found in PRO ED 138/50; *Reading Mercury*, 7 October1939 and *Reading Standard*, 8 December 1939. The Geere House for Tuberculous children of Stepney Green faced similar, though less severe, opposition from householders near Windsor: see GLRO Div. 5 Log Book of the school.

22. Devon Record Office, ARP Evac., Box 11, Folder 115.

23. London County Council, *Interim Report of the County Medical Officer of Health and School Medical Officer for the Year 1939*, pp. 13-14.

24. PRO HLG 7/76, 13 September 1939.

25. PRO ED 50/212, letter to the President of the Board of Education, 9 November 1939.

26. Shropshire Record Office, County Council Bundle System, Evacuation 162, Box 23.

27. PRO ED 136/205; PRO ED 138/50; PRO HLG 7/322.

28. Judith Grunfeld, *Shefford: The Story of a Jewish School Community in Evacuation, 1939-1945* (London, 1980).

29. Bedfordshire Record Office, W/Ev/3.

30. PRO ED 10/246.

31. *North Berks Herald*, 1 December 1939.

32. PRO ED 134/73.

33. GLRO, CH/M/6/2.

34. GLRO, CH/M/6/4.

35. Report in the *East End News*, 28 November 1941.

36. PRO ED 138/26, September 1941.

37. PRO HO 45/18716.

38. PRO HO 45/19065.

39. Mass Observation, War Diaries (W5229), 2 September 1939.

40. PRO HO (P5402), 8 September 1939.

41. Mass Observation, Topic Collection No 5, Evacuation Folder 1/B, 6 September 1939.

42. Mass Observation, Folder I/1, Observer D.4.

43. PRO HLG 7/74, 11 September 1939.

44. *News Chronicle*, 12 October 1939; 13 October 1939; 14 October 1939; 16 October 1939; 20 October 1939; 25 October 1939.

45. Mass Observation War Diaries C5282, W5220, M5376.

46. Mass Observation, T. C. #5, Folder 1/E.

47. Imperial War Museum, Elkus Collection, no date, but probably late 1939.

48. Mass Observation, T. C. #5, Folder 1/E.

49. Imperial War Museum, Elkus Collection.

50. Mass Observation, War Diaries (W5229), 2 September 1939.

51. Mass Observation, War Diaries (05390.0), 31 August 1939.

52. PRO HLG 7/334, 1 March 1940.

53. PRO HLG 7/74, 22 November 1939.

54. Mass Observation, War Diaries (W5220), 7 January 1940; War Diaries (M5376), 22 January 1940.

55. *Birmingham Post*, 26 January 1940.

56. *Yorkshire Post*, 11 January 1940; 13 January 1940; 18 January 1940.

57. *Yorkshire Post*, 12 January 1940.

58. GLRO EO/WAR/1/81.

59. According to a Board of Education report; see PRO ED 134/75, 6 March 1940.

60. *Ibid*., 16 March 1940.

61. *Ibid*., 18 March 1940.

62. Evidence for Wantage may be found in the report by the Association of Architects, Surveyors and Technical Assistants whose survey used Wantage as a model for their recommendations for better wartime use of buildings. Their questionnaire contained 130 questions covering local housing, education, social life, and the like. The survey team spoke with billeting officers, local and evacuated teachers, householders and council officials. A copy of the report is in PRO ED 10/247.

63. Titmuss, *Problems of Social Policy*, p. 394.

64. *Newbury Weekly News*, 15 August 1940.

65. Wiltshire Record Office, Clerks 273/3/46C, Crickland and Wootton Bassett RDC to Min. of Health, 14 March 1940.

66. Mass Observation, Directive Replies, 1940; TC #5, Folder 2/L, *passim*.

67. *Ibid*.

68. Cornwall Record Office, AD 336/21.

69. National Federation of Women's Institutes, *Town Children Through Country Eyes* (Dorking, Surrey, 1940), *passim*.

70. Mass Observation, Directive Replies, 1940; TC #5, Folder 2/K, Observer NB, 8 October1940.

71. *Windsor Express*, 9 February 1940; 18 October1940; 25 October1940.

72. *Ibid*., 14 June 1940.

73. PRO HLG 7/101.

74. For these cases, see *Reading Mercury*, 26 October1940; 23 November 1940; 14 December 1940; *North Berks Herald*, 10 January 1941.

75. This is also Titmuss' judgement; see his *Problems of Social Policy*, pp. 391-2.

76. Bedfordshire Record Office, W/Ev/C/Z.

77. Chuter-Ede Diary, British Library, Add. Mss. 59692, 30 January 1942, pp. 128-30.

78. GLRO EO/WAR/1/127.

79. GLRO EO/WAR/1/106.

80. See *TES* 30 August 1941; 6 September 1941; 13 September 1941; 20 September 1941; 27 September 1941.

81. Bedfordshire Record Office, W/Ev/C.W.V.4. This is part of an informative file of billeting problems kept by the County Welfare and Social Office.

82. *Reading Mercury*, 29 July 1944.

83. *Newbury News*, 6 July 1944; 20 July 1944.

84. *The Times*, 31 August 1944.

85. For these examples, see *The Times*, 15 July 1944; 17 July 1944; 19 August 1944; 30 August 1944.

86. Cornwall Record Office, Education Committee Minute Book, 1940-1946, B/T/86.

87. *East London Advert*., 16 September 1939.

88. *East End News*, 24 November 1939.

89. *East London Advert*., 16 September 1939.

90. Shopshire Record Office, County Council Bundle System, 161A, Box 21.

91. See the eulogy by Charles Graves, Women in Green (London, 1948).

92. Rosalind C. Chambers, 'A Study of Three Voluntary Organizations', in D.V. Glass (ed.), Social Mobility in Britain (London, 1954), pp. 383-406.

93. PRO HLG 7/334.

94. An opinion held in common with Lady Denman of the Women's Institute: see PRO HO 45/17635, Anderson committee Minutes, 21 July 1938.

95. Mass Observation, Topic Collection No 5, Evacuation Folder 2/A, 20 February 1940.

CHAPTER FOUR

Beds Before Desks

The lack of co-operation in the reception areas--so widely recognized at the time--not only put the civil defense program at risk. It was immediately clear that the evacuation also seriously disrupted the education of the evacuees. Uprooted from their classrooms, placed in strange schools and surroundings and without congenial billets, evacuees could not continue their studies properly. This was obviously not the intention of the government. It had hoped to retain educational standards by keeping evacuated schools intact in the reception areas: exigencies of transportation during the evacuation had made this impossible.

As the children debouched at the reception area railheads on evacuation day, buses scooped them up and ferried them to various destinations. Because the bus drivers were under orders to move off as soon as the buses were filled, school units were thus broken up. When the Mary Datchelor Girls' School arrived in Kent, the head mistress, Dorothy Brock, watched in dismay as her pupils were taken to seven different villages.[1] Travelling up to fifty miles a day on each of the next ten days, she collected at Ashford 250 of her 438 students: the rest remained dispersed.

Even where schools were billeted in a single town or village, there was often a shortage of classroom space. Haberdashers' Aske's Girls School, Hatcham, evacuated to Hove, was forced to work in five or six scattered buildings. One form worked in several different private houses; another in the aisles of St. Philip's church; a third in the vestry and aisles of St. Leonard's church (where there was, the headmistress wrote, a table--'a priceless boon'); a fourth form worked in two rooms of a church hall belonging to St. Barnabas; a final form used two large buffets at the Hove Dog-racing Stadium. Attempts at alleviating their difficulty were obstructed by local authorities who refused to allow any changes.[2]

Evacuation conditions were so severe that some schools simply disintegrated. A sad example was the Wickham Lane Infant School of Plumstead, London. Initially evacuated to Maidstone, the school could not find class rooms or adequate billeting. After two weeks, the school transferred to a village a few miles from Maidstone. The school log book takes up the disheartening tale from there. 'Transferred to Grafty Green, Kent, a remote hamlet, very bad billeting arrangements, little acc. in poor cottages, very scattered; school was far from billets on hillside, at Boughton Malherbe, primitive building, no amenities, chn. ate sandwiches in leaking crowded classroom, no hot drink, lobby small, wet clothes not dried. As a result of poor billets, insufficient food, distance to school, severe weather, chrn. returned to London by Jan. 1940. Staff returned gradually'.[3]

Although none of the schools evacuated to Berkshire suffered as badly as Aske's or the Wickham Lane School, there were problems aplenty. The Anglican St. John the Apostle School was divided among six different villages near Wokingham. Head Teachers travelled thirty-five to forty miles visiting the schools. This was also true of the Godolphin and Latymer Secondary School for Girls (Hammersmith): 200 girls were sent to Ascot and Sunningdale; 47 to Eton; 38 to Burnham; and 74 to Taplow. In the Wantage reception area evacuated schools were less badly divided; but they faced overcrowded conditions in classrooms, especially in the smaller villages. Wantage town contained three elementary schools and a boys' secondary school; they received 291 evacuee children in September 1939. The surrounding villages usually had a single all-aged mixed school in two or three classrooms. Even a few additional pupils would be difficult to manage in these conditions. Denchworth, with a total village population of less than 200, received twenty-one infants from the Bow School. Twenty-eight Bow School infants and juniors went to West Hanney (population 283); and twenty-seven to East Hanney (population 506). Similar numbers went to neighboring villages. In all, 282 evacuated children arrived in the villages near Wantage in September 1939. Added to the 291 evacuees in Wantage itself, this gave a total of 573 new school children. These numbers, however, do not include the approximately 100 privately evacuated mostly middle class children, who attended the Wantage district schools.[4] Overcrowded classrooms forced the Wantage area schools--in common with Berkshire and reception areas generally--into a double-shift system, with local children attending at morning sessions and London children in the afternoons. Half-time schooling was widespread in Berkshire as late as December; one school near Abingdon had even less time in the classroom, sharing the village school on alternative afternoons.[5]

Scattered schools and overcrowded conditions in the early weeks of the evacuation brought out a growing divergence of opinion in the government about the disposition of the evacuated children. Events had in fact overtaken planning. So much attention had been given to the military demands for a quick dispersal that later stages of the evacuation were neglected. The problem was compounded by a division of authority in the reception areas. Urban and rural district councils responsible to the Home Office or the Ministry of Health managed billeting, whereas education lay under the local education authorities responsible to the Board of Education. There was little consultation between these groups of local authorities about the long term educational needs of the evacuees. Strictly speaking, billeting authorities acted correctly in rapid and expedient billeting. The aim of evacuation had never been to facilitate education, but to save lives: 'beds before desks' was their motto. Evacuated staff and teachers did not disagree with an initially quick dispersal, but they argued that a second phase must include provisions for the continuation of education among evacuees under their own teachers. Doubtless, reasons of self-interest among teachers were significant in their desire to keep schools together. If evacuated schools merged with those in the reception areas, there was a strong likelihood that evacuated teachers would be made redundant, affecting not only immediate employment but retirement pensions as well.[6] Teachers thought, too, that schools must maintain their cohesiveness for other reasons. Most of the evacuated schools were from the poorer parts of the cities, where schools were recognized centers of social and hygienic improvement. Ambitious working class parents regarded schooling as the key to social mobility for their children. In addition, school medical services played a vital role in maintaining the health of their children. Clearly, if schools were broken up in the reception areas, more than reading and writing would be affected. For all these reasons, it is easy to understand why the preservation of 'school identity' was the first priority of evacuated teachers. During the initial weeks of evacuation, many schools could retain their identity only by engaging in substantial rebilleting. Naturally enough, local residents and billeting officers were unwilling to undertake what amounted to a second evacuation in as many weeks. From their point of view, they had done their job.

As the autumn days of 1939 wore on, other difficulties for evacuated teachers appeared. They acted increasingly _in loco parentis_--supervising the distribution of clothing to the needy, for example, or making emergency visits with pupils to the doctor, dentist, or chemist. Teachers spent more than the usual amount of time comforting and encouraging their pupils. As reception area attitudes toward evacuees became less friendly, teachers devised programs after school hours to relieve householders from too much foster care. Teachers' loyalty to the evacuation scheme also meant that they worked overtime persuading evacuee parents to support the scheme and assuring them that their children were well treated in the billets.

Administrative duties for heads of evacuated

schools also increased. Arrangements had to be made with local schools, churches, or village or borough authorities for the use of available facilities. These often needed repair or alteration: school heads had to supervise. Staffing problems were endemic as teachers joined the forces, or contributed to the war effort in some other way. More intractable difficulties were caused by the evacuation itself. Evacuated teachers were under considerable stress. They had lost familiar laboratories and libraries. Their billeting problems were often no less severe than those of their students. They had left home and family in the vulnerable areas. If teachers had children, there was an added anxiety as they, too, were evacuated. Some teachers became less efficient, demoralized by the disruption of their careers and the dislocation of their families. Teachers were understandably determined to retain what they could of an accustomed routine, of established teaching methods, and of students whom they knew.

Teachers sought redress for their grievances in the first instance from their professional organizations. One of the most active was the London Teachers' Association, a local branch of the National Union of Teachers. Through its official organ, The London Teacher, a campaign was organized against the 'rank injustices' of the 'Dictators in the reception areas'.[7] The President of the LTA, Ella Cohn, condemned the 'mess and muddle of evacuation' and proclaimed that far too often there had been 'professional as well as personal distress and unhappiness' for London teachers.[8] The LTA complained especially about the loss of school identity and of the attempts of local educational authorities who made unreasonable demands on teachers' leisure time. 'Teachers did not sign away their liberty and embrace serfdom when they volunteered for evacuation', as one leading article put it.[9] The LTA, in fact, took a far stronger line against what it considered evacuation abuses than did its parent organization, the NUT, presumably because the NUT represented reception area teachers as well as evacuees.

Teachers also appealled to the Board of Education. They were puzzled and angry to discover that the Board did not always see it their way. The Board's major concern was to return every child to full time education as soon as possible. In some cases, this was most readily accomplished by merging the evacuated units into the village schools, a policy directly contrary to the desires of evacuated teachers. The Board was undoubtedly motivated in part by its concern over lost classroom time; but they were also fearful that householders in the reception areas would revolt if forced to care for evacuees half the day.[10] The full time session was as much designed to take evacuees off householders' hands as it was to promote education. Official dislike of the preservation of school identity did not discourage the evacuated teachers. When requests for support went unheeded, teachers took matters into their own hands by cadging meeting halls and carrying out the necessary rebilleting of their pupils. This provoked further conflict in the reception areas. One Senior Regional Officer complained to the Ministry of Health that teachers were 'raising hell' in his region by rearranging billets and issuing complaints about unco-operative local authorities.[11]

Teachers never ceased to doubt that preservation of school identity was the key to evacuation success. Evidence suggests their view was essentially correct. A sense of unity and continuity among evacuated schools promoted high teacher and student morale. This certainly was the experience of the Cranbrook Terrace School of Bethnal Green, a senior mixed school evacuated to Wellington, Somerset. For the first three months of the evacuation, classes were held in an old police station and in two local schools during off hours. After the Christmas holidays, however, the school found an empty fourteen room house which served far better.[12] Similarly, the Wandsworth School--initially scattered 'by an act of gratuitious folly' (in the words of the headmaster) over several villages near Woking--solved its problem by leasing a large private home, where they lived happily for the remainder of the war.[13] The advantages of group billeting was confirmed in Berkshire by an HMI, who wrote at length about the Cubbit Town Glengall School from Poplar.[14] Originally dispersed among several villages, two units of the school were eventually brought together. One unit of thirty-nine children was billeted at the residence of Lord Faringdon in Buscot Park, and another of thirty-six children was established at Coleshill House. Teachers and helpers lived with the children in what can only be described as an ideal setting. Possibly not every evacuee appreciated the beauty of Coleshill House, designed by Inigo Jones, but the practical features were undeniably attractive to everyone--spacious laundry and drying room facilities, and food prepared by the domestic staff. Buscot Park had similar amenities including a swimming pool and tennis and squash courts. Neither group seemed to mind sleeping in the servants' quarters and eating in the servants' hall.

Special schools particularly benefitted from community living. The Manchester Lancastrian School for Cripples, which evacuated 100 children to the stable block of a large country house near Whitchurch in Shropshire elicited high praise from an HMI, who wrote that the headmistress had managed 'to hold together a willing, happy, hard-working team of domestics, nurses, and teachers' in carrying on the normal activities of the school, including placing her charges in suitable employment when they left the school. [15]

These examples suggest that, even in the face of considerable obstacles, evacuated schools could function reasonably well if they were kept together by a dedicated band of staff and teachers. Of course the cost in time and energy of such an achievement was substantial. Two unique wartime sources document the burdens of day to day management of evacuated schools. Both sources are London school teachers' diaries.

The first diary was written by Dorothy M. Hoyles, head teacher of the Albany Road School in Camberwell, a junior mixed and infants' school evacuated to Weymouth in Dorset.[16] Her story begins in September 1939 and ends in May 1942 when the school merged with several others in Weymouth. From the diary a picture of Miss Hoyles emerges slowly, almost accidentally: indefatigable; tactful; dedicated; wholly scrupulous in her dealing with students, parents, and townspeople.

Not given to hyperbole, speculation, or the spreading of rumors, Miss Hoyles writes with a detached understatement that suggests a calm and realistic eye.

The opening pages of Miss Hoyles' diary reveal that the Albany Road pupils found the transition easy at first. The excitement of Dorset's coastline and beaches brought a holiday mood. This was prolonged during the warm and sunny September days of 1939 because the double shift system necessitated numerous walks along the sea-front during the off sessions. Behind the happier scenes of children frolicking on the beaches, however, staff and teachers were hard at work. They visited every billet regularly and sponsored conferences with hosts on subjects such as bed times, cleanliness, and postcards to parents. Teachers dealt personally with verminous cases, though these were few. Miss Hoyles only once had to bring soap, paraffin, vinegar and a Derbac comb from a local clinic to despatch the most persistent nits at the school.

As elsewhere, some re-billeting in Weymouth was necessary. Teachers arranged transfers under the direction of the local billeting officer. Classroom space for the two hundred or so Albany Road pupils also proved nettlesome. After negotiations with the elders of Ebeneezer Hall for the use of their chapel fell through, Miss Hoyles eventually secured St. Paul's Church. A joyful entry in the diary for 25 September celebrated the event: 'First assembly under a roof!' The church also housed some of the infants. Miss Hoyles pressed her luck too far when she asked the vicar for glebe land as a gardening plot: he refused. School supplies were another worry. Essential stocks remained in Camberwell, and Miss Hoyles returned to London on 29 September to arrange for their transfer. Later, she spent several days in furniture shops searching for a school cupboard. The arrival of a dozen pencils from Dorchester was momentous enough to record in her diary.

The variety of tasks that fell to Miss Hoyles can here only be summarized. Soon after her arrival in Weymouth, Miss Hoyles discovered that the school where most of her students attended classes had inadequate air raid protection. She helped organize a team that dug slit trenches nearby. Once dug, the trenches were found to be inadequately drained: water pooled at the bottom. Miss Hoyles had the fault corrected. She then organized ARP practice, gradually working down the time needed to enter the trenches to four and a half minutes.

During any absence or illness of the teachers, Miss Hoyles filled in, usually taking the class on trips which she made as interesting as possible. There were visits to a local bakery and dairy (free samples followed); to a swannery to study the birds; and once to the marshes to observe the construction of an embankment for a new railway line. She often took students on nature walks as part of their regular curriculum studies. Mindful of her students' needs for religious instruction in trying times, Miss Hoyles took organ lessons from the organist at St. Paul's so that she could accompany her students' hymn singing. On one occasion she taught Beethoven's 'The Praise of God' to children sheltering from a storm in the church.

Friendly relations with the community were important to evacuated schools as Miss Hoyles well knew. She willingly gave interviews to the local newspaper. She took an active role in the Joint Consultative Committee of Weymouth and Evacuated Teachers, established to thrash out better means of cooperation between local and evacuated schools. Most important of all in earning Weymouth's hospitality was the preservation of order and discipline among the evacuees. Miss Hoyles dealt with misdemeanors sympathetically yet firmly. On 21 September, a foster parent brought to Miss Hoyles some articles found in the possession of her four evacuee girls, stolen as it transpired, from Woolworth's and Marks and Spencer. Miss Hoyles and a colleague engaged in active diplomacy with a local J.P. to avert prosecution. The girls returned the articles with apologies. Miss Hoyles begged from the store managers a second chance for the girls: it was granted only 'after special pleading'. Miss Hoyles then found new billets for the troublesome four, not an easy task. There were other cases of this kind. On 3 November, Miss Hoyles escorted several evacuee boys to the Central Police Station for a cautionary tale about window-breaking. On 6 November, she returned to the station, reporting that another evacuee has 'found' 8s 3 1/2d hidden in a wall near the Odeon Picture Palace.

Above all were two pressing problems for Miss Hoyles: the need for full-time sessions; and continuous re-billeting. In the early months of evacuation Miss Hoyles desperately searched for adequate classroom space. By mid-November, the goal was in sight. Various buildings had been patched together for long enough stretches to allow full-time sessions. But suddenly on 18 November, the military authorities comandeered St. Paul's Parish Room, which had been a standby for the Infant's Department. They were now effectively evicted. Even though the vicar, the minister of the Methodist church, and an alderman were arrayed against the commanding officer, they could not free the premises. Eventually the school secured rented rooms in Milton Road for their classroom needs, but not until considerable alterations had been made. Miss Hoyles and a colleague constructed blackout frames for the windows with wood and paper.

Many of her days were taken up with what she called 'billeting and visiting'. In one instance, a foster parent could not persuade her four evacuees to sort out sleeping arrangements so that the two brothers would sleep together in one room, and two sisters in another. Miss Hoyles left her own billet on a stormy night to mediate, successfully, and then returned 'soaked to the skin'. In a different case, Miss Hoyles visited the foster parents of a particularly troublesome pair of sisters already in their fourth billet. After an hour's talk, Miss Hoyles persuaded the foster parents to keep the girls. Billeting duties in some form made an appearance sixteen times in her diary from 9 October to 10 November. Saturday, 11 November, found Miss Hoyles once again on the billeting circuit. She began that day placing two brothers in separate houses because of their continuous fraternal quarrelling. She then visited a foster parent who was concerned about an outbreak of scabies among the evacuees in her house: two boys were sent immediately to the Isolation Hospital. Their places were taken by two others, a good-hearted deed on the part of the foster parents as the new evacuees were eneuretic.

Later in the day, Miss Hoyles took up the request of two sisters, Barbara and Blossom, for an extra blanket. Their brother, Billy, known for his lurid language, had settled down quietly in another billet nearby. But that very afternoon, the mother of the three arrived from London to fetch them home. She objected to the fact that her children had so recently changed billets. 'One cannot please both parent and billetor', concluded Miss Hoyles despairingly.

Miss Hoyles was especially active in dissuading London parents from taking their children home. The first case of this kind on 10 September revealed her strategy. She discouraged the request by referring the parent to the local billeting officer. Unhappily, that official ruled that the choice lay with the parent. Miss Hoyles then wrote the Ministry of Health and the LCC, requesting that further steps be taken. She thereafter made it her policy to speak at length with parents who wanted their children returned.

Only rarely did the diary contain direct criticisms about the evacuation scheme. On 10 November 1939, Miss Hoyles wrote: 'The government seems to be nullifying its own Evacuation Scheme that it has been our daily task to uphold'. Her specific reference is unclear, but seems to suggest the government lacked consistency and firmness in its evacuation arrangements, a fair judgement, as we shall soon see. On 22 November, Miss Hoyles had a conversation with the chief billeting officer of Weymouth, who thought householders could be partially relieved of their burden if the evacuees were rotated monthly. Miss Hoyles firmly rejected such an idea as giving the 'death blow' to evacuation 'which the teachers were doing their best to keep alive'. Apart from these comments, Miss Hoyles gave every evidence of supporting the evacuation: indeed, all her energies were bent on making it succeed. As she confessed to Leah Manning, a NUT representative and former MP: 'it was necessary to live from day to day--even from hour to hour--in order [to] keep going'.

The evacuation experiences of Miss Hoyles were similar to those of another London teacher, who kept a detailed diary in the early years of the war. Miss H.M.W. Williams was head of the infants' department of the Harbinger School, Millwall, evacuated to Abingdon and five neighboring villages in Berkshire. Her diary begins in December 1939 (the early weeks of the diary have been lost) and continues until 1944.[17] The contrast between Millwall, in the docklands of the Isle of Dogs, and the rustic charm of the Berkshire countryside must have been startling. Miss Williams, like Miss Hoyles, showed an admirable adaptability under stress. She was obviously capable, enthusiastic, and untiring in the interest of her students. Again like Miss Hoyles, she was careful to touch all the proper social bases. In December 1939, she sent Christmas greetings and expressions of thanks to foster parents, helpers, church ministers, clinic staff, and borough officials--125 cards in all. She contributed to the Abingdon Mayor's Christmas Fund. In 1940, she sent Easter greetings from the school to all foster parents. Clearly, Miss Williams went out of her way to associate herself and the school with the life of the borough.

Miss Williams' reception area difficulties sound familiar, though they were compounded by inadequate heating in the church hall used for classes in that first cold winter. The months of December 1939 and January 1940 were the harshest in half a century. It was so cold in late December that the Cherwell froze over at Oxford. In Abingdon, the lavatories froze in the rooms used for classes by the Harbinger School. The problem continued for weeks on end. The diary notes laconically on 17 January 1940: 'Cistern in lavatory frozen so Miss Williams and helpers set to work to thaw it'. Once thawed, the pipes and cistern frozen again within a few days. Miss Williams and a colleague spent most of the morning of 22 January thawing the cistern, but failed with the pipes. That afternoon, 'Miss Williams and Miss Burn again at the cistern and pipes'. On the days when ice rose in the toilets, they could not be used by the students who had to be dismissed. Tardy coal deliveries exacerbated conditions. In fact, prodding the local coal merchant was a standing necessity. Miss Williams once sent four boys and a trolley to fetch enough coal for the day.

On 27 January, Miss Williams inspected the lavatories and found a joint in one of the pans leaking. She immediately called it to the attention of a trustee and informed him of the general state of the church's plumbing. Four days later, she rang local officials about the lavatory. On 3 February, it was discovered that a coke stove in an upper room was unsafe. In the meantime, work had begun on the lavatories: new ones were used for the first time on 8 March. On 22 March 1940, a new coke stove was installed to celebrate the advent of spring. For Miss Williams, it had been a trying winter.

As was true with other evacuee teachers, Miss Williams assumed an increasingly parental role with her students. Arbitrating between foster parents, evacuees, and townspeople stretched to the limit her capacity for tact. In a typical case, two girls came before her because they were 'so naughty' and told lies. While assuring the foster parents, Miss Williams punished the girls by withdrawing their privileges at Country Dancing and Guides. On another occasion a London evacuee decided to walk home. Miss Williams changed this determined little girl's mind by showing how she was helping the war effort in the reception area. In an instance of what appeared to be an incorrigible case of juvenile kleptomania lasting over many months, Miss Williams spoke frequently to affronted shop owners, reimbursing at least one of them from her own pocket. She re-billeted the boy several times--once into a clinic for observation. Finally, she wrote the boy's parents and the London Probation Office: he was sent home in January 1942. Throughout the whole episode, Miss Williams displayed exemplary patience and kindness.

Of such small dramas was the evacuation made: their successful resolution contributed significantly to what contentment there was in the billets and to the preservation of some educational continuity among the evacuees. This was certainly true of the Albany Road and Harbinger Schools: they bore their evacuation in reasonable order. Their success, as we have noted, can be attributed in large part to the teachers and staffs of the schools. They dealt humanely and sensibly with their evacuees under trying circumstances. In addition, they showed managerial and practical skills of a high order. If we generalize from these limited samples, we may understand how important the role of teachers was to the long term continuance of the evacuation. Evacuated staff and teachers were, in a sense, the foot soldiers of evacuation; they were on the ground, directly responsible for the day to day advance of the evacuation scheme.

From our discussion thus far, it is clear that evacuated teachers were wholly absorbed in making the evacuation work under the most adverse conditions. They had time for little else. They certainly lacked the leisure for reflecting on the prospects of the future development of education, or for experiments in new curricula. It seems unlikely that we can look to the main body of evacuated teachers for any impetus to educational reform. Yet both wartime contemporaries and later commentators have claimed that teachers led the movement for educational reform.[18] It has been held that the evacuation, by breaking the traditional molds of educational practices, prepared the way for post-war educational changes. It was assumed in the early days of the evacuation that urban teachers, thrust into the countryside, would be forced to improvise and alter their methods of teaching. The evacuation would provide new and exciting pedagogic opportunities. Teachers would familiarize their classes with nature at first hand and thus spur an interest in biology; or give new meaning to history by examining castles or country houses on location. The Board of Education, in its wartime pronouncements, encouraged this line of thought. In November 1939, the Board declared that the evacuation gave the schools a chance for 'personal initiative and resourcefulness', by challenging them to 'jettison unreal teaching, to look outside at real things rather than at apparatus indoors'. Furthermore, the evacuation provided a setting 'for teachers themselves to learn something, in new conditions, from the open minds of their children'.[19] But the Board was indulging in unreal hopes: there is a hint of wishful thinking in such pronouncements. Perhaps understandably, the Board as a government department took a charitable view of the evacuation and its likely effects upon education:

after all, their job was to assure the success of the evacuation.

Even if teachers did not find themselves overburdened with evacuation responsibilities, they could hardly have been expected to profit automatically from finding themselves in a new environment. Some preparation would have been necessary. Many teachers lacked the special skills, knowledge, or interest that would allow them to take educational advantage of their country rambles. They often roamed about on 'field trips' with students simply because they had to fill time. Nor were their students always interested. Miss Williams of the Harbinger School, a keen nature lover and amateur botanist, encouraged her students to collect and learn the names of wild flowers. To her disappointment, she discovered that the students disliked walking and were uninterested in flowers.

The absence of a significant reform movement led by evacuated teachers is born out by one of the few wartime surveys specifically addressed to the question of educational experimentation. C.R. Rawson examined 104 London schools in May 1941.[20] All of his respondents were head teachers. Most of the schools were elementary. Rawson discovered that although there were some attempts at experimentation in the early months of evacuation, they quickly faded as the heavy duties of evacuated teachers pushed aside any thoughts of curriculum reform. Among a sample of sixteen London schools evacuated to Berkshire, few reported any experimentation. What changes there were tended to be some form of nature study. For example, gardening was popular. But even gardening seemed less self-consciously reformist than a necessary adaptation to local conditions. This was true of other subjects as well. Science in the evacuated schools was often agricultural science. Admirable though this may have been, it did not necessarily represent a turn toward 'real things'.

That there would not be a spontaneous reform among the hard-pressed evacuated schools was eventually recognized by the Board of Education. In a report issued in late 1940, the Board confirmed mounting evidence from the reception areas that the evacuation had hindered educational progress. HMI evaluations of wartime educational conditions in elementary schools around the country admitted that only during the first phase of evacuation, before the fall of France in June 1940, were there opportunities for an adventurous approach to education.[21] Subsequently, teaching conditions became less favorable. As one district inspector put it: 'Jack-in-the-box changes to which schools have been subjected during the past 15 months were not conducive to new developments'. In some regions 'an unsettled attitude to schooling' had developed. R.H. Charles, chief inspector of elementary schools, summed it up dispiritedly: 'There has appeared a tendency to return to a more formal kind of teaching; there is less experiment and adventure, and some of the freer and interesting methods of teaching which were familiar before the war have been given up'. In junior schools, too, curricula had suffered substantially, becoming 'narrower, duller and more formal' than before. Only among some seniors may there have been some slight gains in gardening, cookery, history, and geography.

An LCC report confirmed that wartime conditions had adversely affected the schools.[22] The report reviewed the results of a test given in 1943 to two thousand elementary students. Originally devised in 1924, the test provides for a comparison among generations of students. Although students continued to write lively English compositions, their spelling was poorer when compared with the students of 1924. In arithmetic, history, and geography, the 1943 attainment was 'appreciably lower' than in 1924. In the face of such evidence, it seems doubtful that the evacuation in itself advanced the cause of educational reform.

If evacuee teachers cannot be seen as educational reformers, they nevertheless played an important role beyond the classroom during the evacuation: they became the most important voice for evacuee grievances. School children and their mothers who had been deposited in the reception areas had no others to whom they could readily turn. Teachers were quite willing to listen and to help. They had suffered indignities during the evacuation no less than their pupils. Rawson relates a representative anecdote of two teachers who arrived late on evacuation day at a mansion near Reading. Tired from their day's duties, they were ushered through the dining hall--elaborately set for an evening meal--to an outlying building in the garden where six boys had already been installed. The teachers were then given their first meal since early morning, a pint of tea and a loaf of bread. They were bedded down with mattresses on the floor. Another story related by Rawson tells of the late arrival of two head teachers at the house of a prominent reception area resident. The hostess declared it was too late for tea, forcing them into the unfamiliar, blacked-out town for a meal. Incidents such as these suggested to teachers that they were victims of class discrimination. True enough that many teachers were members of the working class; but they considered themselves as upwardly mobile professionals.[23]

The ill will that grew in the reception areas between host and evacuee, as recorded in this and the previous chapter reached such proportions that evacuees began to desert the evacuation program in large numbers by late 1939. They preferred the distant prospect of bombs to the realities of billet life. Evacuees returning to the cities added further strains imposed upon wartime education as schools found their students divided between evacuation and reception areas. More importantly, peripatetic evacuees brought the entire evacuation scheme under risk, threatening the linchpin of the government's evacuation policy. How the government attempted to meet the threat is the subject of the next chapter.

NOTES

1. M. Dorothy Brock, 'An Unusual Happening: The Story of The Mary Datchelor Girls' School in Evacuation, September 1939-May 1945'. (Privately printed, no date.)

2. See PRO, ED 134/73.

3. GLRO, D.O. 6 Wickham Lane School Log

Book, 'I', 1933-1959.

4. Numbers are taken from the Association of Architects Survey, PRO ED 10/247.

5. PRO ED 134/19 contains a Board of Education memorandum setting out Berkshire school conditions district by district in December 1939. As late as April 1940, over 4000 Berkshire children were without full-time education.

6. A fear voiced in *The Schoolmaster*, 19 October 1939.

7. *The London Teacher*, 13 October 1939.

8. *Ibid*., 27 October 1939.

9. *Ibid*.

10. PRO ED 10/246, 21 December 1939.

11. PRO HLG 7/76, 11 October 1939. The report came from Nottingham.

12. Dorothy Isabel Martin, 'Evacuation Justified', a brochure, tells the story: a copy is in PRO ED 138/36.

13. The history of the school during evacuation can be pieced together from *The Link*, the school magazine. Copies are at the GLRO, EO/WAR/5/13.

14. PRO ED 134/256, 4 November 1939.

15. PRO ED 138/36.

16. The diary is in manuscript at the Imperial War Museum, LS. Box No. 77/50/1 Miss D.M. Hoyles.

17. The diary is in manuscript at the GLRO, EO/WAR/5/1.

18. See, for example, the work by the editor of the *Times Educational Supplement*, H.C. Dent, *Education in Transition* (London, 1944); and P.H.J.H. Gosden, *Education in the Second World War* (London, 1976).

19. PRO ED 136/205, 13 November 1939.

20. C.R. Rawson, 'Pied Piper'. In typescript at the Greater London Council History Library, County Hall. By matching raw questionnaires with coded numbers, it is possible to identify both the schools surveyed and the official who made out the questionnaire.

21. PRO ED 138/34.

22. LCC Education Committee, 'Standard of Attainment in London Elementary Schools' (London, 1943).

23. GLRO, EO/WAR/1/83, 22 April 1940. Report of a conference between the LCC Education Office and the London Schoolmasters' Association.

CHAPTER V

Government Under Attack

The previous two chapters demonstrated how the evacuation scheme became unpopular during the early months of the war. In this chapter we examine the government's response to its faltering policy. Parliamentarians, civil servants, and ministers discussed the difficulties at length. We should not over-emphasize the time taken up with evacuation at the highest governmental levels. After all, there was a war to win. But the serious implications of a break-down of the evacuation scheme were clear to everyone.

The government faced two fundamental difficulties. First, by not committing itself firmly to an active administrative role in the implementation of the evacuation, the government appeared weak, indecisive, or insincere even to its supporters. Second, the government was hindered by a policy which proved to be contradictory: educational aims conflicted with civil defense objectives. These problems tossed evacuation officials to and fro.

Opposition to the working of the government's evacuation scheme was most dramatically revealed during a parliamentary debate in the first days of the war.[1] Criticism crossed party lines. Roughly speaking, Labour members represented urban evacuation areas, and Conservatives with some Liberals served as spokesmen for reception areas. All sides spoke against the evacuation. A common theme among the reception area MPs was the repugnance they (and their constituents) felt for the evacuees. Sir Henry Fildes, the National

Liberal MP from Dumfriesshire, in an echo of familiar reception area attitudes, castigated the government for forcing into the homes of private British citizens 'persons suffering from venereal disease, scabies, and all sorts of infectious complaints'. Major Owen, Liberal member for Caernarvonshire, declared it 'ludicrous' for evacuees to be sent to the beautiful Welsh countryside which had only 'quiet country public houses', unsuitable for the roistering urban working class. Owen also read a report from a group of Welsh billeting officers criticizing evacuees' hygiene and health. He hoped fewer evacuees would be sent 'among people with whom they have not sympathy, whom they cannot understand, who are entirely different from them, who speak a different language, have different habits, and have different thoughts'. The Conservative member for western Aberdeenshire, Captain Thornton-Kemsley, used more abusive language. He deplored the 'indescribable' behavior of some evacuees whose 'primitive habits' had caused the destruction of householders' carpets, mattresses, and bedding.

Conservative and Liberal attacks upon the evacuees brought hot replies from a small group of radical members of the ILP, the so-called Red Clydesiders. Campbell Stephen, member for Glasgow Camlachie, charged that 150 evacuees at Inverary had been put into a 'miserable, cold hall' containing only two lavatories, while the nearby residence of the Duke of Argyll with numerous bedrooms had scarcely been used. The Duke had taken in only a few evacuees, housing them in his basement. George Buchanan, member for Glasgow Gorbals, who had a reputation in the House for straightforward speech, took direct aim at Captain Thornton-Kemsley. 'I am not having the children whom I represent slandered', he declared angrily. 'They are as good as yours, and I am not having them slandered in a superior tone'. Buchanan was brought to order by the Speaker only with difficulty.

More moderate voices from the Labour side also defended the evacuees. Haden Guest, member for Islington, told the House that in his long experience as a medical doctor in the poorer parts of London, he had never seen any evidence of primitive habits. Evacuee behavior in the reception areas was a psychological problem. Their ignorance of country ways and their sudden separation from familiar home life could incite antisocial behavior. The Rev. R.W. Sorensen, Labour member for Leyton West, agreed. Working class women accustomed to their own homes would find it difficult to be in the home of a stranger. A way must be found, he suggested, of assuring them they had not been dumped and forgotten in the countryside. Cooler heads thus prevailing brought a restrained tone to the concluding stages of the debate.

The government no doubt regarded the results of the debate with some equanimity. Opposition speeches were shrugged off. Even backbench criticism from normally friendly forces could be tolerated easily enough: expressions of anger might usefully seem as a vent for constituency frustrations over evacuation problems. But events outside the House were more disturbing. As disenchantment in the reception areas grew to an uproar, evacuees retreated. They came home. From a trickle in the early weeks of September, evacuees leaving the reception areas reached a flood by the end of 1939. More than 77,000 children from London alone returned before the year's end -- one third of the children who had gone out.[2] Other cities outside London encountered comparable numbers of returning evacuees. Unless the trend were reversed, the whole of the government's civil defense program could be imperilled.

There was a second danger, as we have noted earlier. On evacuation day, schools were closed and compulsory education abandoned in the belief that cities would be without children. Returning to the cities, children found themselves without educational opportunities and with little to do. The loss of schools, the break-up of neighborhood ties, and for older children, the lack of jobs in the early chaotic days of the war promoted a sense of disorientation and malaise. An additional problem was the decline of school medical services. The health and hygiene of children from the poorest families was directly threatened. By late September, growing numbers of unkempt children appeared in the streets of the larger cities. An LCC social worker, visiting one of her cases in Hammersmith, reported crowds of 'dirty, neglected-looking children, playing about aimlessly'.[3] A district inspector of schools observed hundreds of children 'running about idle all day' in the Isle of Dogs.[4] Some children spent much of the time in cinemas or amusement centers -- concentrations which could hardly have been considered safe refuges during bomb attacks.

Expressions of concern about the impact of evacuation upon education reached the Board of Education with increasing frequency. By late 1939, the Board had received discontented delegations from local labour parties, the Industrial Women's Organisations, the National Council of Women, and the National Union of Teachers. As might be expected, among the most vocal critics were the evacuated teachers in the reception areas. Typical was the lunch time talk among teachers from a New Cross school evacuated to Burwash, Sussex, who deplored the reports of children 'running wild' in the streets of London. In their opinion, the government was destroying in seven months an educational system that had taken seventy years to build.[5] A Walthamstow teacher, evacuated with his school to a village near St. Albans, urged decisive action. The whole business was 'a farce', he wrote: 'we lose kids every week. The Government must vacillate no longer -- either evaucation or not: no half measures: close all schools in Walthamstow or open them and admit their failure'.[6] The headmistress of the Lady Margaret School in Parson's Green evacuated to Haslemere wrote in a tone beyond exasperation: 'We should be glad to be informed whether the Government really considers Education of any importance whatever, and whether they really intend the evacuation of schools to continue or not. The action of almost all their officials right through this business leads one to suppose that neither matters very much either way'.[7] Private schools were no less critical of the government. Although they had rarely participated in the government's evacuation scheme, private schools were directly affected by the government's blanket closure of schools in the cities. They consequently bombarded the Board of Education with requests to re-open.

Attacks in print were also beginning to appear with some frequency. Lady Simon's pamphlet, 'The Children in War-Time', published by the WEA in December, cogently outlined the failures of evacuation and the breakdown of education. *The Journal of Education* was vehement in its criticism. 'That education should be in its present state of chaos is little short of a national disaster', it claimed. 'The Government should act, and act at once'.[8] Perhaps the most widely read criticism of the government's policy in these early days was a series of articles by Ritchie Calder in the *Daily Herald*. Calder visited London and several provincial cities. He described the boredom and growing sense of hopelessness among urban children: evacuation was not, he assured his readers, a happy holiday. Children were 'starved of education, numbed through lack of direction, and neglected in health'.[9] The series -- called the 'Dead End Kids' after the popular movies of the time -- brought to a wide readership the problems of evacuees who returned to the cities. Calder reinforced his observations by writing directly to the Board of Education about the physical and moral deterioration he had seen in the East End of London.[10] Calder was not, of course, entirely disinterested. He was a member of the Labour Party ARP Committee and a leading journalist for an opposition newspaper. His book, *The Lesson of London* (1941), severely critical of the government's civil defense measures, was surely motivated in part by political reasons. Nevertheless, there was much truth in his observations of life in the evacuation areas.

The chorus of criticism was bound to have an effect. Indeed, the government was not insensitive to the problems. Walter Elliot, Minister of Health, professed himself disturbed by the appearance of London 'street Arabs'.[11] The government had no wish to undermine the welfare of future generations: they were determined that the school medical service should survive the war intact. They also realized that every day the number of evacuees declined in the reception areas, the greater the sense of grievance among householders who had retained their evacuees. Participating householders could feel unfairly burdened and 'the relics of an unsuccessful scheme', as one Ministry of Health official put it.[12]

Both Elliot and Lord de la Warr, president of the Board of Education, worked closely together on solving the 'drift back' problem. Conferences between health and education officials took place with increasing frequency during the autumn of 1939. The Civil Defense Committee of the War Cabinet, presided over by Sir John Anderson, discussed the problem several times. Compulsory evacuation was mooted but rejected as impractical. There was some concern that the evacuation scheme could fail completely. On 24 October 1939, therefore, the Civil Defense Committee authorized the Ministry of Health, the Board of Education and the Secretary of State for Scotland to begin planning in secrecy a second evacuation scheme (eventually known as Plan IV) which would be implemented during actual air attacks.[13] Only bombs, it was thought, would drive the evacuees back to the billets. In the meantime, the government mounted a campaign of persuasion against drift back: it was directed at evacuees and their parents.

To implement the campaign, de la Warr employed a variety of tactics. He enlisted the aid of C.H. Middleton, a popular gardening speaker on the BBC. By portraying children happily engaged in country pursuits, Middleton might convince parents to remain with the scheme. Middleton's co-operation was cloaked in secrecy. If it were suspected that he mouthed official propaganda, Middleton could lose some of his large gardening public. After de la Warr was given the intended script beforehand for vetting, the talk was duly given in November. Among his gardening tips, Middleton urged evacuee mothers to keep their children in the country. Now was the time, he reminded them, when school gardens should be planted. Children remaining in the countryside had 'a golden opportunity' for new interests which would be 'a sweetening influence' remaining with them all their lives. 'Very sentimental stuff', admitted Sir Bernard Maconachie, the BBC's Director of Talks; but he also thought Middleton did 'this sort of thing without being nauseating'.[14]

De la Warr next wrote Lady Marion Hyde, a lady-in-waiting to the Queen, asking if the Queen would be willing to visit an evacuated school.[15] Lady Marion replied affirmatively and the Queen appeared at Horsted Keynes, near East Grinstead. De la Warr then requested aid from the Ministry of Information: they recommended a series of BBC talks by such voluntary bodies as the Boy Scouts, Girl Guides, Salvation Army and Toc H who would speak well of evacuation.[16]

These attempts at propaganda were ineffective: there was no reduction in the rate of drift back. In retrospect, the Board's efforts seem amateurish and unconvincing. Perhaps they suffered the same disadvantage of distance from their public that characterized the Ministry of Information during the early years of the war.[17] Very likely the Board did not understand the depth of mutual antagonism that had developed between evacuees and householders. Nor did it seem to grasp completely the strong bonds that drew families together and led mothers and young children back to the vulnerable areas. An East End newspaper was blunt in its criticism of the government's campaign: 'scolding the parents or little stories with big morals on the wireless will be of small help'.[18]

Something more substantial than propaganda was necessary to salvage both evacuation and education. Unfortunately, there was no clear course of action. If the Board of Education provided schooling for returning evacuees, it would encourage drift back and thus undermine further the government's civil defense policy. If it did not reopen schools, the Board would come under increasing pressure for abrogating its educational responsibilities. The government hit upon a compromise solution: it opened so-called emergency schools in the vulnerable cities. Limited in hours and curriculum, these schools accommodated children eleven years and older who lived within a mile of the school. Attendance was voluntary. The government thus hoped, by restricting classes and pupils, to prevent them from becoming a magnet for evacuees who remained in the reception areas. At the same time, the schools could at least provide basic educational needs for a few children who had returned to the evacuation areas.

In announcing the creation of emergency schools on 1 November 1939, de la Warr declared that they had become necessary because of returning evacuees. In effect, he blamed the evacuees for the problematic course of the evacuation. Evacuees, he warned, should return immediately to the country: 'if raids really come, there can be no nice and orderly evacuation as before; there will just be a rush and everybody will have to take his chance'.[19] This was not true, as de la Warr was well aware. The government had already begun planning for another evacuation. Perhaps he hoped scare tactics would work.

The day after de la Warr's announcement in the Lords, Elliot tried in the House of Commons to ease parliamentary unrest about evacuation. Half the mothers and 78% of the children who had been evacuated were still in the reception areas, Elliot declared. This was, he claimed, proof the scheme was 'striking root' everywhere -- a remark received sceptically by the House.[20] Nor did Elliot's reassurance remove doubts in the countryside. A leading article in the *Birmingham Post* noted that Elliot's defense of evacuation suggested 'a success rather greater than many observers, no enemies to the scheme, would find evidence to justify'.[21]

The Board had hoped the emergency schools could be made available immediately; but this proved impossible. At the outbreak of war, many schools had been commandeered for military and civil defense purposes. Among London's elementary schools, for example, over 250 had been taken by the Auxiliary Fire Service, 100 had become wardens' posts, seventy were first aid decontamination centres, and several dozen more served as ambulance depots, feeding centres, or mortuaries. Reconverting schools would take time. In addition, the LCC moved slowly in establishing emergency schools, believing that schools should remain closed until adequate civil defense protection could be provided. This was a reasonable line of argument; but de la Warr and his permanent secretary at the Board, Sir Maurice Holmes, requested quicker action from the LCC. It was of 'vital importance' wrote Holmes, that as many London schools as possible re-open 'at the earliest possible moment'.[22] Sir Wilfred Eady at the Home Office exerted added pressure on the LCC. He advanced the curious argument that lack of protective works should not delay the opening of schools because such works were designed largely for 'psychological reassurance'.[23] These remarks from de la Warr and senior civil servants suggest they were under an urgent ministerial mandate to respond to their critics.

Unfortunately for the government, the emergency school program was criticized from the outset as inadequate. During a parliamentary debate on education in November 1939, members on all sides of the House called for a return of school buildings for educational purposes and for a restoration of educational standards.[24] The attack soon widened into an assault on the Board of Education. The Liberal Sir Percy Harris declared the Board lax from the beginning. Leo Amery, a Conservative, urged a bolder policy. His Conservative colleague, Vicountess Davidson, feared that education and discipline among children would both be lost during the war unless the Board acted quickly. The sharpest word of the day came from George Tomlinson. He spoke with authority as the newly elected president of the Association of Education Committees, representing the directors of education throughout the country. He accused the Board of having 'failed lamentably' in the present crisis. 'Instead of giving a clear, definite lead it has spoken in a lame, halting voice, when it has spoken at all', Tomlinson charged. He also predicted that the approaching Christmas holidays would 'prove the zero hour for evacuation'.[25]

De la Warr himself viewed Christmas with despondency. He confided to Elliot that the holidays may well be the death of evacuation 'unless Hitler play[ed] up with a bomb'.[26] As parents and children drew together at this traditional time of year, drift back was bound to increase. Even if evacuees returned home with the idea of only a temporary visit, families would part with their children reluctantly at the end of the holidays. To counteract the anticipated surge in drift back, the Civil Defense Committee of the

War Cabinet devised a program which encouraged local authorities in the reception areas to sponsor Christmas treats, paying for them through the rates or by voluntary contributions. If evacuees were feted well enough, perhaps they would remain in place. Along with the carrot of Christmas treats, the government showed the stick of dissuasion. Shortly before the holidays, the government announced it would make no special Christmas transportation arrangements for the evacuees or their parents. This mean-spirited declaration was reinforced in the House of Commons by Prime Minister Chamberlain himself, who urged parents to keep their children in the countryside.

The Christmas campaign began with movies, pantomimes, parties, and musical festivals in the reception areas. Pictures and stories of happy evacuees filled the columns of local newspapers. The LCC responded admirably by establishing a Christmas fund of 5000 pounds to help defray expenses incurred by local authorities. The campaign at first seemed moderately successful. There was no massive exodus from the reception areas. But after Christmas, drift back continued. More than 3000 children returned to London each week in January. The campaign had proven only a temporary expedient.

By January 1940, evacuation seemed near collapse. The Association of Education Committees predicted the government would soon concede defeat.[27] The Association's official organ, Education, concluded: 'The evacuation scheme, as originally contemplated, has crumbled to pieces in the hands of the Government'.[28] The cost of failure was high. Twenty million pounds had been wasted; education in the reception areas was largely improvised; there had been no schooling at all for upwards of half a million children since September. The only solutions, Education believed, were compulsory evacuation, more central co-ordination, and less voluntarism in the scheme generally.

The government, however, was unwilling to abandon its voluntarist approach, especially when this suggestion seemed to emanate mostly from its opponents on the left. The government was nevertheless forced into an important policy change. Its earlier premise that the evacuees were at fault for the failures of evacuation was no longer tenable. An important memorandum drawn up in January 1940 by those ministers most responsible for evacuation made a significant admission: evacuation was failing less because of obduracy of evacuees than the recalcitrance of rural hosts.[29] The evidence was incontestable. Reception area householders and billeting authorities were 'very tired', the memo sadly noted: 'the element of good will on which the initial success of the scheme depended has diminished and in some districts disappeared'. The inescapable conclusion was that a re-direction of evaucation propaganda was needed -- away from the evacuees toward the rural householder. The task of working out the details of the new policy was given to Sir John Anderson's Civil Defense Committee.

Throughout January and February, 1940, the Committee deliberated ways of reviving the flagging evacuation program. To solicit information and advice, the Committee called an evacuation conference in late January. In attendance were leading ministers, representatives of local authorities (including the LCC), and the NUT. At the conference the government heard its conclusions confirmed. In an official statement, the LCC declared the entire evacuation program was 'endangered' primarily 'through lack of co-operation of the foster parents and often of the billeting officer'. Securing new billets had become 'a matter of outstanding difficulty'.[30] The LCC could draw upon hundreds of experiences in substantiation of its argument. Other educational bodies supported the emerging consensus. Resolutions passed at a conference of Head Masters and Head-mistresses in January 1940, recommended that the government cease its appeals to parents of evacuees. Instead, the government should call upon householders in the reception areas for 'a generally wider spirit of forbearance and understanding in their acceptance of the children's presence'.[31]

Ideas generated at the evacuation conference and among committee members led to the development of three broad strategies for saving evacuation. First, there would be a new evacuation scheme, as envisioned by the Civil Defense Committee in October: as agreed then, it would not be brought into play until air raids were underway. It would differ from the original evacuation scheme by omitting certain categories of the population -- the aged, cripples, and mothers of young children -- and be limited to school children, some children under five, and expectant mothers. Evidence from the evacuation areas suggested that these groups made more desirable guests. Additional relief to the original reception areas was given by diverting substantial numbers of future evacuees to south Wales. This did not meet with everyone's approval. The LCC's education officer, W.J.O. Newton, thought it unfair that billeting should be extended to poorer regions, such as the depressed mining communities of the Rhondda Valley in south Wales, while affluent Worthing, Ware, or Letchworth were let off relatively lightly. He believed the government had made this decision to avoid compulsory billeting in the wealthy shires.[32]

The government's second strategy was a new propaganda effort centered on the reception areas. Elliot, the Minister of Health, rapidly took up the cause and by late February 1940, could report that 'a persistent stream of propaganda was being maintained and almost every householder was getting something through his letter-box'.[33] He also planned a wide use of press, radio, and personal letters. Newsreels and posters were under consideration with the Ministry of Information. Propaganda alone would be inadequate, as the government realized. More tangible benefits were necessary to some rural hosts. Elliot announced to the House of Commons increased billeting allowances for evacuee children fourteen years of age and over. Special hostels for 'unbilletable' and difficult children would be established. As a royal sweetener, the Queen would send personal messages to householders keeping evacuees. Most important was a spring campaign, consisting of a series of county conferences between evacuation officials and local authorities to iron out remaining evacuation problems.

The government's third strategy dealt with the growing numbers of children in the evacuation areas. De la Warr announced on 7 February 1940 that as soon as schools could be made safe, compulsory education would be re-imposed. Thus, all children in the cities, not merely those voluntarily attending emergency schools, must return to classes. It was a tacit admission that the emergency schools had failed after a three month trial. The return to compulsory education was a decision no doubt reluctantly taken. As we have noted earlier, it contradicted the evacuation policy in general and more specifically it weakened the new scheme still in its planning stages. But the government had little choice. It could no longer preside over the collapse of the country's educational system. Only a week before de la Warr's announcement, Kenneth Lindsay (de la Warr's parliamentary secretary) had been forced to admit in the House of Commons that more than 400,000 children in the country were without formal education.

The re-imposition of compulsory education in the cities did not win the government any laurels. Head Mistress Dorothy Brock's incredulous reaction was doubtless typical among teachers: 'That the Government which was still urging parents to keep children out of dangerous areas, should ... . undermine its own evacuation scheme, is one of those workings of the official mind which I confess I find it hard to follow'.[34] Press comment was mixed, but generally critical. In a leading article, <u>The Times</u> demonstrated its sympathy with the government's dilemma: de la Warr's decision showed the choice 'must be made between the uncertain risk of bombing and the certain risk of deterioration among the children'. The <u>Daily Express</u> and the <u>Daily Telegraph</u> were harsher. The <u>Telegraph</u> condemned the government's education policy of the past five months as 'one of the most deplorable examples of waste in all the national war organisation'. The <u>Express</u> agreed: the Board 'had thrown up the job'. The <u>Manchester Guardian</u> drew the obvious conclusion. 'We have had five months of voluntaryism', it wrote: 'we see where it has brought us'.[35]

As schools re-opened in the cities, the new evacuation scheme, Plan IV, simultaneously went forward. The scheme required registration of potential evacuees: more than 550,000 were expected. By early April, 1940, after weeks of publicity, only 95,000 had registered; 842,000 had not even replied to the registration request; more than 220,000 had refused outright. One Divisional Officer explained it thus: 'Parents have heard about and can imagine the horrors of a bad billet more easily than the horrors of an air raid'.[36] The sad truth for the government was that even if more had registered, sufficient numbers of billets were unavailable; for the spring campaign to win over the reception areas had also failed.

Central to that campaign, it will be remembered, was a series of county conferences where representatives from the Ministry of Health and the LCC spoke with local authorities and billeting officers. Minutes of these meetings held in March and April of 1940 made painful reading for the government.[37] In Northamptonshire, householders were 'very unwilling' to accept further evacuees. In Oxfordshire, Lord Macclesfield, chairman of the County Council, extensively criticized the scheme. At the Soke of Peterborough meeting, chaired by the Marquis of Exeter, there was 'great hostility' about the new scheme: one critic remembered that 75% of the original evacuees were 'unsuitable'. Rutlandshire delegates closely quizzed the LCC representatives in attendance about the districts from which any new evacuees may come. Herefordshire officials doubted that enough billets could be found under Plan IV. Opposition was 'very pronounced' in West Suffolk and every district council representative objected to the numbers of evacuees alloted under the plan. In Leicestershire, the LCC representative was questioned about the medical inspection procedures under Plan IV. The Norfolk meeting reported the 'utmost difficulty' in securing additional billets. Berkshire's reluctance to receive more evacuees was given voice by one of its MPs, Sir Ralph Glyn. He openly sympathized with his constituents' dread of a repetition of the September evacuation. In any case, he wrote, Berks was 'practically saturated' with evacuees.[38]

Continued reception area hostility made it

plain that even the government's last resort of compulsory billeting was probably unenforceable. A Senior Regional Officer predicted that the 'present temper of the countryside' would prevent billeting officers from acting, for they could not afford 'to make enemies of the whole town or village'.[39] This gloomy view was substantiated by evidence of a growing dissatisfaction among billeting officers. Threats of resignation among them became commonplace in the wake of the spring campaign. After a third billeting officer had resigned in a local Berkshire community, the district councillor asserted that billeting officers too often got 'more kicks than halfpence'. Some billeting officers were becoming militant. A protest meeting of Bucks billeting officers in March, 1940, condemned evacuation as 'unsatisfactory' because it placed an 'unreasonable strain' upon householders.[40] Life for a billeting officer had become a troubled one.

Faced with a barrage of criticism from householders in the reception areas and opposition from crucial voluntarist officials such as billeting officers, as well as the loss of support among evacuees themselves, policy makers once again took up the topic. In a rare show of annoyance, Sir John Anderson confessed that the whole problem of evacuation 'was getting increasingly difficult and complicated'.[41] So much so, as he informed the Civil Defense Committee, that it had been necessary for the Foreign Secretary to obtain a release from the French government from an earlier obligation admitting 200,000 refugees from France. Adding a foreign element to the billeting problem was unacceptable.

The government's unresolved dilemmas over evacuation and education gave a continuous opportunity to its parliamentary opponents. Labour members stepped up their criticisms during the winter of 1940. The Board of Education, as before, drew most of their fire.[42] One MP charged the Board with shirking its duty and showing 'great weakness and vacillation'. Another condemned the Board for having 'taken everything lying down' and acting submissively before the other ministries. A third agreed that the Board was the 'Cinderella Department of the

Ministries'. The Board's political weakness within the existing government was most accurately outlined by the labour member for Abervon, W.G. Cove, a Rhondda Valley radical and former miner who was also an official of the NUT. Reminding the House that both de la Warr and his parliamentary secretary, Lindsay, were National Labour members of a predominantly conservative ministry, Cove jokingly confessed to the House that he had been longing 'for a good, blue-blooded Tory' to take their place because they were 'politically the weakest pair of Ministers in the Government'. They had 'no following, no power, no influence'. Cove's remarks about the political weakness of the President of the Board of Education voiced an open secret. Nor was it any secret that de la Warr was unhappy with Chamberlain's policies -- as he often admitted to Harold Nicolson.[43] De la Warr had first served in Chamberlain's cabinet as Lord Privy Seal, but had been demoted to the Board after he objected to the policy of appeasement at the time of Munich.[44] Though it is difficult to see what de la Warr could have done to enhance the Board's policies in the light of the cross-currents of evacuation, his days in office were numbered.

The failures of the government's evacuation and education policies were soon overshadowed by events on the continent. The phoney war was coming to an end. The German advance into Norway, the attack on Belgium and Holland and the Luftwaffe's first, tentative probing of British defences brought home the failure of the policy of appeasement. Chamberlain's resignation in May 1940 and the formation of Churchill's coalition government signalled a revitalization of wartime preparations. This logically meant a stronger civil defence effort and a fresh attempt at bringing order to the evacuation scheme. Given this task were the new Minister of Health, Malcolm MacDonald, son of the fallen Labour leader, and Herwald Ramsbotham (later Lord Soulbury) at the Board of Education. Know as 'Tups' to his initimates, Ramsbotham had been Minister of Pensions from 1936 to 1939 and First Commissioner of Works from 1939 to 1940 before his promotion to the Board. He had served the Board earlier as parliamentary secretary from 1931 to 1935 and had been well liked. Baldwin thought him one of the coming men of the Conservative Party. His eye glass and double first at Oxford may have seemed formidable, but Thomas Jones reported him as 'quite human'.[45]

Although Ramsbotham's tenure at the Board was brief, there was considerable movement in the evacuation program--even some measure of success--in response to the German military threat. As the Germans advanced rapidly across northern France toward the Channel, preparations were made to repel an expected invasion of England's eastern counties. The government also devised several experimental evacuation schemes.[46] In May and early June 1940, the government instituted a 'special scheme' which removed non-essential citizens within a ten mile zone extending inland along the coast from Norfolk southward to Sussex. London children evacuated there in 1939 were re-evacuated to South Wales and the Midlands; local children followed soon after. Other citizens were urged to move inland. Schools in the region closed. The government issued travel vouchers and billeting allowances for the needy. As a result of the government's program during the summer of 1940, almost sixty percent of the population in the affected coastal towns left for the interior. The prospect of invasion overcame their distaste--temporarily--for the evacuation. This 'special scheme' had been set in motion before Plan IV was operating; the latter, as we will remember, was to begin only when air raids were in progress. But when the news of further German advances reached England in early June, the government initiated Plan IV immediately. Between 13 and 18 June, 103,000 children left London.

For late registrants to Plan IV, Plan V was devised. Also known as the 'trickle' evacuation, it sent out weekly trainloads of unaccompanied children from London. Plan V was given added impetus by E.G. Savage, the LCC's Education Officer, after he experienced at first hand life in one of London's public shelters.[47] Savage was convinced that the unhygienic conditions in the shelters harmed the health of children. Determined 'on some real propaganda' to promote evacuation, he organized a campaign of personal visitation in London to hasten evacuation among the remaining children. School inquiry officers visited homes and public shelters, speaking to parents and holding meetings. The results were not encouraging: only 33,051 agreed to register. More than 60,000 were not at home to the surveyors; even more disheartening, more than 100,000 refused outright to register.[48] Overall, only 64,000 were evacuated under Plan V.[49] It was suspended in 1942 because, as a Ministry of Health official admitted, of the 'increasing reluctance of householders to receive evacuees'.[50]

Of all the evacuation schemes launched during the crisis of 1940, the overseas program excited the most attention world-wide. Prompted by offers of help from private citizens in the Dominions and the United States, the government established in June 1940 the Children's Overseas Reception Board. Chaired by Geoffrey Shakespeare, then under Secretary of State for the Dominions, CORB rapidly mobilized evacuees who wished to go abroad during the course of the war. Those eligible were children between the ages of five and sixteen who attended a grant-aided school in England and Wales. There were also stringent health requirements for overseas evacuees. Children with defective teeth had to have dental treatment before their application could be forwarded. Children suffering from scabies, impetigo, or pediculosis must be completely cured before applying. If a child's eyesight was bad enough for spectacles, this, too, had to be remedied. There was no charge to the families for the sea voyage. Planning and processing of the applications worked Shakespeare and his CORB staff day and night--ninety hour weeks were not uncommon.[51] The response was strong: 210,000 applications were received by 4 July when CORB announced that no further requests could be taken. Shakespeare estimated that 94% came from working class families.

Successful applicants (largely determined by medical inspection) could go only if there were available passenger space. Unfortunately, the very day that the scheme was approved, 17 June 1940, was the day that France surrendered. The French fleet went to the new Vichy government, putting added pressure on the Royal Navy and reducing its ability to keep the seas free from U-boat attack. Unless the safety of the evacuees could be reasonably guaranteed on the perilous north Atlantic run, the government could not underwrite the scheme. There were two alternatives for a safe crossing. Evacuees could either go on fast, unescorted single ships or in convoy on slower ships. The War Cabinet decided on the latter course to assure survivor assistance in case of submarine attack. Weekly consignments of children began arriving at ports of embarkation for convoy crossing before the end of July. Soon after, the first overseas evacuees had safely reached their destinations.

There was a widespread initial approval of the scheme both at home and abroad and it gave an active sense of participation in the war effort among the host countries. On the other hand, there were fears that the example set by CORB might prompt a mass exodus. Britons in flight from their besieged country could give German propaganda a field day. Rear Admiral Sir Tufton Beamish, the backbench conservative M.P. for Lewes and member of a distinguished naval family, made this point several times in the House of Commons. He thought that overseas evacuation could produce 'despondency and alarum' at home. He also claimed that in his part of Sussex, 'panic and evacuation' had already begun among the 'wealthy and leisured classes', who were evacuating themselves and their children 'all over the country'.[52]

Beamish's statement was surprising--and came from a surprising source. But he had strayed onto the most controversial topic of overseas evacuation. There were unsubstantiated reports that wealthy and influential families buying passage on departing ships did so at the expense of the poor, who had to wait for the slower working of the government scheme.[53] It was certainly true that those who could pay and were willing to take the risk crossed the Atlantic when they wished. Whether or not this was at the expense of places that could have gone to the poor was difficult to determine. In any case, the government was eager to scotch the rumour, for Lord Haw Haw had charged that CORB was benefitting the rich.

In a seven hour debate on 2 July 1940, Shakespeare defended the scheme before the House of Commons. CORB was pledged to choose a cross-section of children, favoring no particular class. The numbers were as large as the program could comfortably manage. CORB was not simply transporting children from one country to another: it was part of a grander imperial scheme. 'These children will form friendships, contacts and associations in the Dominions, and the silken chord which binds the Empire together will be strengthened beyond all power to sever'.[54] Clement Atlee, then Lord Privy Seal in the wartime coalition, defended the scheme more prosaically as an extension of civil defense, always at the heart of evacuation. The House seemed satisfied with the government's explanation, with the possible exception of Rear Admiral Beamish who warned, prophetically as it happened, that the Germans would without hesitation torpedo a children's ship.

Within a fortnight the overseas scheme was again at the center of a parliamentary controversy, caused by the sinking of the Arandora Star off the west coast of Ireland. The ship was carrying 1500 Italian and German internees to Canada, many of whom were opponents of fascism. The lesson drawn from the sinking of a noncombatant vessel was obvious: no ship could be called safe. Four days later, the War Cabinet decided to cancel its overseas programs.[55] Private arrangements could go forward unhindered. Atlee's announcement of this decision provoked two days of angry reaction in the House of Commons. James Griffiths, Labour MP for Llanelly, told the House of the 'great resentment' in his constituency because children of 'responsible public men' had been sent overseas while 'poor children' were left behind.[56] Griffiths declared that the common people did not ask 'for anything more than the ordinary protection which everyone else gets, but they resent it and feel indignant if rich people are looking after their own children and allowing the children of the poor to stand all risks'. It must be, he said, 'a really democratic Britain for which we fight'. A Conservative from the East Riding agreed: anything that savored 'of class distinctions' should be 'ruthlessly stamped out'. A Liberal member recommended the cessation of private overseas arrangements. The Labour MP, George Tomlinson, thought equality of sacrifice implied equality of risk. Kenneth Lindsay, having slipped his muzzle after losing official status in the recent cabinet reshuffle, also attacked the class discrimination which the overseas scheme had revealed. 'More and more', he said, 'this is a people's war if ever there was one'.

The uproar forced Churchill himself on the following day to modify the government's position. The overseas scheme had only been postponed, not abandoned, he assured the House. Furthermore, any future overseas evacuation would be regulated 'with a view to restoring the balance between classes'.[57] Thus, Churchill implied, even private overseas evacuation would come under government scrutiny. As a result of Churchill's pledge, CORB's life was extended.

As we now know, parliamentary critics of overseas evacuation had not overstated their case. Home Office papers reveal the substantial truth of discrimination in the overseas program. On 10 July 1940, Sir John Anderson wrote to Chamberlain (still a member of the cabinet) of the bad feeling that would be aroused in the country 'if the children of well-to-do parents continue to go overseas in large numbers'.[58] Geoffrey Shakespeare had the facts at his command. During June 1940, ten thousand passengers left for the dominions: of these, 2,345 were children. Except for a handful, all came from affluent families.[59] Shakespeare was genuinely concerned about the imbalance of classes among the overseas evacuees, and felt a strong sympathy for the underprivileged. Perhaps his earlier associations with Lloyd George, for whom he was once private secretary, gave him a radical tinge. The only signs of panic and alarm among applicants for overseas evacuation, he observed, were among a large number of public schools, many of whom planned evacuation en masse. But, said Shakespeare, there had been no sign of 'unreasonable alarm' from the 'very many letters we have received from working class parents'.[60] When Shakespeare reviewed the passenger lists for July 1940, he saw further evidence 'of the rich swarming overseas'.[61]

Shakespeare's concern with the inequity of the overseas evacuation was revealed in a series of negotiations with Sir John Anderson and Ronald Cross in the Ministry of Shipping. Between them, they hoped to iron out the imbalance of classes. Before details could be completed, a disaster at sea brought to an end any hope of a continued government sponsored overseas scheme. On 13 September 1940, the 11,000 ton City of Benares, originally built for the India run, left Liverpool for Canada with 400 crew and passengers. Among them were ninety children and nine adult escorts. The ship travelled in convoy, with flanking ships in the event of an attack. By 17 September, the convoy was 630 miles out and beyond the zone of greatest danger. The convoy dispersed, each ship going its own way. Within twenty-four hours, a torpedo struck the City of Benares in the children's quarters. High seas delayed the launch of the lifeboats. The ship sank within twenty minutes. Only one hundred were saved, including two CORB escorts and seven children. One of the escorts, Mary Cornish, kept up the spirits of the Lascar crewmen and children in her lifeboat by telling endless variations of _The Thirty-Nine Steps_ and _Bulldog Drummond_.[62]

Heroism and courage at sea, however, was not enough to save CORB. On 30 September the War Cabinet cancelled the program. This proved to be a timely decision. Six hundred children set to disembark at Glasgow were recalled: one of the ships they were to have sailed on was sunk within twelve hours of departure. From the government's point of view, the end of CORB removed an embarrassment. It is difficult to see how the desired balance of classes among overseas evacuees could have been practically worked out.

NOTES

1. Hansard, House of Commons, vol 351, 14 September 1939.

2. These are official numbers from the LCC: see GLRO EO/WAR/3/5.

3. MO War Diaries (N5382), 17 October 1939.

4. GLRO EO/WAR/3/12, 19 December 1939.

5. MO War Diaries (M5376), 13 February 1940.

6. MO Topic Collection No 5, Folder I/D, 6 November 1939.

7. PRO ED 134/74, 3 December 1939.

8. _The Journal of Education_, 1 November 1939, p. 687.

9. _Daily Herald_, 26 October 1939.

10. PRO ED 10/246, 26 October 1939.

11. PRO ED 50/207, 26 October 1939.

12. PRO HLG 7/90, probable date of December 1939.

13. PRO CAB 73/1, minutes of 24 October 1939.

14. For this episode, see PRO 138/50, 24 October and 31 October 1939.

15. PRO ED 10/246, 26 October 1939.

16. _Ibid_., 13 November 1939.

17. As discussed by Ian McLaine's _Ministry of Morale_, (London, 1979).

18. _East London Advertiser_, 14 October 1939.

19. Hansard, House of Lords, vol 114, 1 November 1939.

20. Hansard, House of Commons, vol 353, 2 November 1939.

21. _Birmingham Post_, 3 November 1939.

22. GLRO EO/WAR/3/9, 17 November 1939.

23. GLRO EO/WAR/3/43, 2 November 1939.

24. Hansard, House of Commons, v. 353, 16

November 1939.

25. *Ibid.*, cols. 931, 939. Tomlinson was the first Minister of Education in the 1945 Labour government.

26. PRO ED 136/125, 18 October 1939.

27. *Education*, 19 January 1940, p. 46.

28. *Ibid.*, 16 February 1940, p. 131.

29. The memo may be found in PRO ED 136/112, 9 January 1940.

30. GLRO EO/WAR/1/82, 18 January 1940.

31. GLRO EO/WAR/1/65, 22 January 1940.

32. GLRO EO/WAR/1/183, 13 February 1940.

33. PRO CAB 73/1, minutes of 21 February 1940.

34. Brock, 'An Unusual Happening', p. 13.

35. See *The Times*, 8 February 1940; *Daily Telegraph*, 8 February 1940; *Daily Express*, 13 February 1940; *Manchester Guardian*, 8 February 1940.

36. GLRO EO/WAR/1/79, March-June 1940.

37. GLRO EO/WAR/1/81.

38. *North Berks Herald*, 8 March 1940.

39. PRO HLG 7/75, 1 April 1940.

40. GLRO EO/WAR/1/84, 19 March 1940.

41. PRO CAB 73/1, minutes of 12 June 1940.

42. The following debate may be found in Hansard, House of Commons, vol 537, 17 February 1940.

43. De la Warr was cousin to Nicolson's wife, Vita Sackville-West, and had been responsible for securing Nicolson a parliamentary

seat in 1935 as a National Labour candidate.

44. Ian Colvin, *The Chamberlain Cabinet*, (London, 1971), p. 261.

45. Thomas Jones, *A Diary with Letters 1931-1950*, (London, 1954), p. 150.

46. A detailed account of the evacuation schemes in 1940 will be found in Titmuss, *Problems of Social Policy*, ch. III.

47. GLRO PH/WAR/1/19, 15 September 1940. Savage (1886-1981) was responsible for the post-war London comprehensive schools. See *The Times* obituary, 20 May 1981.

48. GLRO EO/WAR/1/48.

49. PRO ED 10/248.

50. PRO HLG 7/114, 8 December 1941, P.H. Barter to SRO, Birmingham.

51. See Shakespeare's autobiography, *Let Candles be Brought In*, (London, 1949), ch. 13; and his obituary in *The Times*, 11 September 1980.

52. Hansard, House of Commons, vol 362, 2 July 1940, col 662.

53. McLaine, *Ministry of Morale*, p. 96.

54. Hansard, House of Commons, vol 362, 2 July 1940, col 714.

55. PRO HO 186/343, 6 July 1940.

56. See the debate in Hansard, House of Commons, vol 363, 16 and 17 July, 1940. Griffiths became the Minister for National Insurance in the 1945 Labour government.

57. Hansard, House of Commons, vol 363, 18 July 1940, col 394.

58. PRO HO 186/343.

59. *Ibid*., 25 July 1940.

60. PRO HO 186/343.

61. *Ibid*., 21 August 1940, to Sir John Anderson.

62. Elspeth Huxley, *Atlantic Ordeal: The Story of Mary Cornish*, (London, 1941).

CHAPTER VI

An American Interlude

The Children's Overseas Reception Board was only one example of a diverse series of plans set in motion when the bombs began to fall throughout Europe in 1940. The initial trickle of homeless civilians in the early days of the war rose to a flood as the German army marched in the wake of the air attacks. The special plight of refugee children caught the attention of countries not yet directly involved in the war. By the summer of 1940, several private and public organizations in Canada and the United States were at work to rescue European children from the dangers of war. Inevitably, evacuees from Britain benefited most. A bond of common sympathy between North America and Britain; close business, family, and academic contacts; and the relative ease of transport all contributed to a larger contingent of British evacuees to North America than from any other country.

The most important of the refugee organizations was the United States Committee for the Care of European Children. Registration for British evacuees under the auspices of the U.S. Committee began in London in July, 1940, and ended in October. The Committee worked with the Children's Overseas Reception Board. During these few months, 3538 children signed on for overseas evacuation. Increasing dangers of trans-oceanic travel and the sudden dissolution of CORB, however, prevented all but 838 British children from arriving in the United States under the sponsorship of the U.S. Committee.

Within the United States, the Committee served as an umbrella organization for a variety of groups: these included charities such as the Salvation Army and the American Theatre Wing of the Allied Relief Fund. In so far as possible children's groups were brought over intact. Fifty-four children, for example, of the Actors' Orphanage in Chertsey, Surrey, came together to the Edwin Gould Foundation in New York.

Numerous American business corporations devised their own schemes for transporting their British employees and families. The Hoover Vacuum Cleaner Company brought to Canton, Ohio, eighty-four British children from the Hoover works in Perivale. Most of the children lived with American employees of the firm. Similarly, the Kodak Company of Rochester, New York, sponsored 156 children of its Harrow employees. Warner Brothers of London sponsored 47 children of its British employees. In like manner, dozens of colleges and universities opened their doors to evacuee families from Europe.

Apart from these large-scale organizational efforts for the evacuees, individual families who could afford the fare sent their children to relatives or friends in the United States and Canada, or even farther afield. This bore out Geoffrey Shakespeare's belief that England's wealthier and most influential families were the most active in securing a safe haven for their children. Given their rank in society and their connections, they would naturally be more successful in sending their children overseas. But this was not without criticism. In an echo of parliamentary debates on the class discrimination of CORB's program, the press and the public were especially outraged at the dispatch to Canada of John Julius Norwich, the young son of Duff and Lady Diana Cooper. Among the complainants was a deputation from Hoxton and Deptford mothers who wished to register their disapproval in person to Lady Diana.[1] At the time, Cooper was Minister of Information, and it was surely a lapse of judgement that his son should be sent abroad.

Yet the decision to send children abroad must not be seen as a simple exercise in class privilege. The conflict between patriotic duty, parental love, and family responsibility was acute whether in rich families or poor ones. Perhaps emblematic of many families was the experience of the author and prominent peace movement leader, Vera Brittain. At first, she was determined that her family would remain in England. In a letter of 4 September 1939 to a friend in New York, she wrote that her two children, John and Shirley, were at boarding schools in the country far from likely bomb threats. During the increased bombing attacks of the summer of 1940, Brittain changed her mind. In an agonizing series of letters the track of her decision can be followed.[2] Her daughter's school was now subjected to air raids and warnings; and her son's school received notification that it would likely be commandeered for a military hospital. No longer safe, and their education soon to be disrupted, the children would fare better abroad. Brittain decided to send them to America. She and her husband saw John and Shirley off from Liverpool on 26 June 1940. It was a distressingly poignant moment that Brittain ever after remembered. 'The small gallant figures which disappeared behind the flapping tarpaulin', she later wrote, 'have never grown up in my mind, for the children who returned and eventually took their places were not the same; the break in continuity made them rather appear as an elder brother and sister of the vanished pair'.[3] Perhaps in an attempt to assuage some of the guilt she may have felt in taking advantage of a privileged position, Brittain volunteered for work at CORB in July, 1940: Geoffrey Shakespeare was her cousin.

The stories of the evacuees abroad are as varied as those evacuees in Britain who went from town to country.[4] But the general sense is that evacuees sent abroad had a friendlier reception. Perhaps class distinctions were less in evidence in North America; and it is certainly true that the evacuees sent abroad were more carefully selected. A few specific examples of overseas evacuation programs can demonstrate easily enough the contrast between the overseas and the domestic evacuation program.

Among the more fully documented of academic schemes to bring across English evacuees was that founded at Yale University in June, 1940--just as the Battle of Britain had begun. The heating up of the war galvanized support for Britain at Yale. Spontaneously among several faculty and other members of the Yale community emerged the idea of sponsoring a group of British academic children.[5] The Yale faculty was circularized and within a few days, 300 places in faculty homes and among New Haven citizens had been promised for prospective evacuees. A fund for the expected expenses raised $10,000. Soon a Faculty Committee for Receiving University Children began organizing the details of the operation: among its most active members were Sidney Lovett, University Chaplain (who chaired the Committee); Dr. John Fulton of the Yale Medical School; and Prof. S.B. Hemingway, the Master of Berkeley College. By inviting faculty families from the Universities of Oxford and Cambridge to New Haven for the duration of the war, the Committee hoped to save (in Dr. Fulton's words) 'at least some of the children of the intellectuals before the storm breaks'.[6]

The Committee cabled C.K. Allen, Warden of Rhodes House, Oxford, and Sir Montagu Butler, Master of Pembroke College, Cambridge. But the Committee's invitations met with a mixed response. Cambridge turned down the offer. Sir Montagu wrote that very few were thinking of leaving England. 'A good many people are opposed to the idea of evacuation altogether', he wrote, 'as they think it savours of alarm'. Some believed, he noted further, that no special arrangements should be made for university children, 'since this might be interpreted as privilege for a special class'.[7] Opposition to an overseas evacuation among academics was not limited to Cambridge dons. At Oxford, the historian A.J.P. Taylor condemned the plan as 'an unseemly scramble'.[8]

Oxford, however, accepted Yale's invitation. Preparations went forward, and 125 mothers and children from Oxford faculty families set sail for Canada in July, 1940. They were accompanied by Canadian and American Rhodes Scholars, lending an official air of a rescue mission. Upon their arrival in Canada, the children were met by members of the Royal Canadian Mounted Police. It was a gratyifing reception. Travelling by train to New Haven, where they were again warmly welcomed, the evacuees were soon sorted out into various faculty and citizens' homes.

The difference between the accommodations of the Oxford evacuees at Yale and those of the mass of evacuees in Britain was striking. From a report drawn up by Dr. Fulton in 1940, presumably to reassure Oxford husbands that their wives and children were in good hands, one can catch a glimpse of the relatively plush life of the overseas evacuee.[9] One evacuee mother and her children, the report related, had found a comfortable five room apartment 'in a good modern neighborhood'. The mother was profitably employed, with the help of a part time nurse for her children, in working on a faculty member's research. Two evacuee children had been placed in a 'lovely suburban home in a new neighborhood'. Two others were living in a Yale professor's 'lovely quiet home...on a breezy hillside'. Another girl was with two Yale psychologists in a 'comfortable home in a well-to-do neighborhood'. A boy was placed with the Trust Officer and Chairman of the Board of Directors of a New Haven bank. A brother and sister were with a prominent member of the Yale Medical School and his wife. 'Both are...definitely well-to-do and live in a very comfortable neighborhood'. A mother and her son were 'comfortably situated' with a more humble graduate student and his wife, though Fulton hastened to add that the graduate student came from 'a wealthy old New York family'. One boy seems to have drawn the plum of the New Haven hosts, a Yale faculty member (and graduate of Yale) who came from 'a prominent Chicago family' and whose wife claimed 'an equally prominent family' in Rochester, New York. Perhaps overstating the obvious, Dr. Fulton emphasized their 'background of wealth and culture'. An added attraction was their 'delightful summer home on Nantucket Island'.

Perhaps it was not surprising that many of the evacuees were favorably taken by the United States. How the glamorous life of American hosts could have affected the evacuees is amply borne out by Anthony Bailey's account of his evacuation.[10] From his home in a 'poky bungalow' near Portchester, Hampshire, where his father was the clerk-in-charge of a two-man branch of the National Provincial Bank, Bailey went to Dayton, Ohio, at the age of seven. He was sponsored by the Boston Daily Transcript evacuation scheme, which had advertised for children of 'professional and clerical' families.

From the first, Tony was struck by the 'largesse of America'. His hosts in Dayton were the Spaeths. Otto Spaeth was an energetic entrepreneur who bought and sold companies; he was also with his brother the largest shareholder of the Pabst Brewing Company. Most impressive to Tony was the house where he spent the next four years. Otto was fond of gadgetry and the latest home improvements. The house was large, 'a mansion', as Bailey remembered it decades later. Apart from the more expected rooms such as kitchen, bedrooms, dining and living rooms, there was a maid's room, a powder room for guests, a governess' room, a butler's pantry, a billiard room, and a special laundry room. The sheer number and variety of plumbing apparatuses was astonishing: sinks, toilets, baths, and showers abounded. Each bedroom had its own bath. The amount of water cascading from these appliances was no less remarkable. In England, the king had set the example by sitting in only four inches of water in the royal tub; but in Dayton, Ohio, there was no limit. One could almost swim in the depths. The standard English geyser for producing hot water--slowly--out of an ungainly crooked spout was put to shame.

In the dining room, the table was 'gleaming mahogany'. Goblets and finger bowls reflected the light thrown by the candles accompanying the meals. On the walls hung the pictures of the substantial Spaeth art collection, including a Picasso, a Corot, a Hopper, and two Gaugins. The diversity of eating utensils placed upon the table seemed as prodigal as the water that coursed throughout the house.

Otto Spaeth was affluent, even by American standards. He was also a public-spirited philanthropist not unlike many of the Yale faculty members. They could easily absorb a few evacuees into their lives. Butlers and maids could manage the most difficult chores. Perhaps this explains why the overseas evacuees enjoyed a more pleasant time away from their homes. Only hosts wealthy enough to provide material benefits to their wartime guests could overcome the potential disadvantages of educational and domestic disruption. Tony, at least, seems to have suffered very little homesickness and developed a strong attachment to the way of life in America.

Apart from the life style which they may have set as a model for young Tony, the Spaeths also represented a freer society, one in which the ideal of manipulating an environment, whether natural or social, was a practical attainment. Near the end of his reminiscences, Bailey sums up these early years in America: 'I got from Otto and Eloise a belief in the perfectability of life....In cardplaying terms, one should now and then shoot for the moon'. This seems to have been a common experience among overseas evacuees.

It would appear that the overseas evacuees saw their evacuation in America as a standard of comparison for the life they left behind in England. Further evidence of the effect of the overseas evacuation upon British schoolchildren can be found in the papers of Ernst Papanek.[11] A leading organizer for refugee relief before the war, Papanek had wide interests in all aspects of the refugee question. He was apparently instrumental in devising a questionnaire sent out after the war to refugee agencies, teachers, social workers, and former evacuees. Responses from eleven evacuees are preserved among the Papanek Papers; they are surprisingly informative about the life they found in America and its impact upon their own lives.

A fifteen year old girl, who described herself as a 'cash girl' in 1947, had been evacuated in October, 1940, to relatives in the United States. Her father was a postman, her mother--as was true in every case among this sample of evacuees--a housewife. She liked the United States and hoped to return. As she put it: 'I think America more modern in most respects'. Another former evacuee, whose father was a lawyer, was by 1947 in university. She had left England in 1940 under the *Boston Transcript* scheme, returning to England four years later.

She remembered the evacuation as a 'tremendously exciting adventure' and her time in America as a 'thoroughly good experience'. Most of her comments were related to her educational experiences. In fact, what she most liked about America was her school. She liked especially what she called the 'adult attitude' toward new pupils and 'progressive education' for older school children. Agreeing with her evaluation was a male evacuee, in command of a postal unit with the army in Palestine at the time of the questionnaire. Evacuated with a group of children whose fathers were employees of the London branch of the Chase National Bank of New York, he was 'eternally grateful' for the evacuation because it allowed him to experience at first hand the freedom of expression and behavior in American schools.

An equally happy evacuation was enjoyed by a twenty-one year old receptionist and housewife. Her father was an 'exhibitor' with Warner Brothers Film Company, and she was evacuated under the Warner Brothers Evacuation Scheme. She attended a convent school in New Jersey, describing it as 'the most beautiful experience of my life'. She professed to miss it 'very badly'. Her American school experience was in direct contrast to overly strict English schools, where she 'never got on well'. Another school girl of fifteen, whose father was the director of a carpet company, thought that schooling was more conventional in England than in the United States--although she thought American schools less advanced than English ones. Her sister of nineteen, evacuated with her, believed, too, that American schools was less snobbish than English schools. Two other sisters, evacuated to Newburgh, New York, had similar experiences. Their father was a bank clerk. The younger sister, by 1947 attending an English grammar school, often missed the life in the United States: 'we were given the best of everything', she wrote. Her older sister, at sixteen soon to begin work as a shorthand typist, liked the amiability and informality of American schools. A twenty-two year old former evacuee found that his stay in America altered his life profoundly: he became an American citizen. His father was an advertising consultant. Also evacuated under the _Boston Transcript_ scheme, he attended both public and private schools in

America. Although American schools he found less advanced academically than English schools, they offered a 'freer type of life'. American schools, he thought, were more humane. 'Reasoning takes the place of beatings and Democracy is impressed upon all students'.

The most thorough response to the questionnaire was given by a nineteen year old student, who was preparing under a private tutor for Oxford or Cambridge entrance. Her father was a company director of a City of London firm. She, her younger sister, and her two brothers (both at Eton in 1947) were all evacuated to friends of her parents. Attending a private boarding school in Connecticut, she found it of equal quality to her English school. Her main complaint against the English schools was that they were hampered by petty rules and regulations. In America, students were treated with more respect. In her efforts to attend university, for example, she encountered unexpected difficulties: 'there is so little opportunity for women to go to college over here', she wrote. 'My years in America have made me resent this'. In spite of her complaints, she could never cut herself off entirely from England. 'After all, with good old English patriotism, it is my country. What I should like to do is effect a few reforms in it, all the same'.

These representative samples seem typical of overseas evacuees. Most came from middle class, or lower middle class, homes--a higher social grade than the majority of the internal evacuees in Britain. Their fathers were black-coated workers, small business men, or skilled artisans: there was also a sprinkling of professional and substantial business interests. But no matter what their background, they were in agreement about the advantages of the American secondary educational system. The idea that English education could be changed for the better was implanted in a small, but significant portion of the wartime population. An even greater sense of urgency about educational reform was growing among those internal evacuees who had never left Britain. This subject is taken up in detail in the following chapter.

NOTES

1. Cooper, Trumpets from the Steep, pp. 53-57.

2. Vera Brittain Archives, MacMaster University, Hamilton, Ontario, Canada; 'Replies June 1940'.

3. Vera Brittain, Testament of Experience: An Autobiographical Story of the Years 1925-1950 (New York, 1981), p. 257. See also Vera Brittain, England's Hour (New York, 1941), ch. 8.

4. See the anecdotes in Carlton Jackson's Who Will Take Our Children? (London, 1985).

5. Diary of John Fulton, Yale University Medical Library, vol XIV, 17-23 June 1940.

6. Yale University Archives, Merle Witkin, 'The Evacuation of British Children to the United States During World War II', Yale Prize Essay (1979), p. 6.

7. Yale University Archives, YRG 6B, Box 2, Folder 6, Butler to Hemingway, 27 July 1940.

8. A.J.P. Taylor, a Personal History (New York, 1983), p. 154.

9. Yale University Archives, A. Sydney Lovett Papers, Box 55, Folder 528, Typescript Report, October 1940.

10. The following paragraphs are drawn from Anthony Bailey, America, Lost and Found (New York, 1980).

11. Ernst Papanek Papers, New York Public Library, Box 11. At the time of the questionnaires, in 1947, Papanek was Director of Child Projects, Unitarian Serivce Committee in New York City.

CHAPTER VII

Evacuation and Educational Reconstruction

During the early months of the war, education for the nation's children was widely perceived as the greatest wartime casualty. The evacuation had seriously disrupted schooling, as we have learned in detail. Once emergency schools were opened in some of the larger cities in 1940, thus reversing the flow of the evacuation, educational disruption was given an added dimension. It was now dangerous to attend urban schools. School buildings were large and inviting targets, especially for small 'tip and run' bombing sorties. Hundreds of schools had suffered damage by the later years of the war. Some schools opened and closed as the air attacks dictated. The Langford Road Infant School in West London, for example, which had originally been evacuated to Cambridge, returned as an emergency school in April, 1940. Although it undertook extensive ARP work, it was severely damaged in September, 1940, and closed until May, 1941. The Peterborough Mixed School, also in West London, had a similar history. Established as an emergency school in April, 1940, it was so severely damaged by incendiary bombs in June that it reopened only in October, 1941. The Devons Road emergency school in the East End closed on 16 June 1944, when a nearby blast blew out the windows. On 26 June, it reopened but closed after three days to allow further repairs. On 3 July, it again reopened, but closed within a fortnight after further damage by enemy action. It remained closed for the summer. During this period of heavy raids, school attendance at Devons Road was very low, averaging only six percent.[1]

Low attendance was typical of schools reopening in the evacuation areas. Of 100,000 children in London in November, 1940, only about twenty percent regularly attended classes. Low attendance was also common in those school districts adjacent to London: East Ham (32.5%), Dagenham (48%), and Willesden (59%) seem typical.[2] The worst bombing incident of the war involving an LCC school was at Sandhurst Road, a junior mixed and infants and senior girls' school in Lewisham. On 21 January 1943, just at noon, a single bomb fell from an abortive large-scale German raid. Before exploding, the bomb penetrated all floors of the building. Twenty-four infants were killed immediately in the dining hall; another fifty were taken to hospital. In all, forty-two died, including six teachers.[3]

By late 1940, cities other than London experienced the impact of the raids upon education as the Luftwaffe turned its attention from the capital to the north and west. On 14 November 1940, the first raid on Coventry occurred. Shortly afterward, Birmingham, England's second largest city, was heavily bombed. After a succession of night-time bombings, approximately 20,000 Birmingham children were evacuated. Of the 80,000 children who remained within the city, many had no schools to attend. Forty schools had been severely damaged; another one hundred had minor damage, such as windows blown in and roofs holed--enough to interfere with classroom work. Full-time schooling in Birmingham was temporarily at an end.[4] The same story could be repeated wherever the German air attacks spread throughout late 1940 and into 1941: from the northern industrial and commercial centers of Manchester and Liverpool to the southern ports of Southampton, Bristol, and Portsmouth. Typical was the experience of the Northam Girls' Elementary School in Southampton. Severe air raids began interrupting classes in September, 1940. On 19 November, the school was closed entirely so that neighborhood homeless could be fed on the premises after a particularly extensive air raid. On 25 November, the school playground was cratered during a bombing run. In further raids on 30 November and 1 December, the school building was damaged. On 3 and 6 December, school was dismissed because its staff was involved in war-related work.[5]

There was a similar story in Bristol. This great port city had at first been designated a neutral area: it neither sent out nor received evacuees. Instead, it served in the early months of the war as a conduit through which evacuees passed from London into neighboring villages and towns. On 24 November 1940, however, began the first of many large-scale and sustained raids on the city and its port which altered its status to an evacuation area. The schools were immediately affected. School log books recorded the impact of the bombing. At the damaged Brislington School for Boys, only four scholars were present the day after the raids: the school closed. The Windmill Hill Infant Boys School had suffered a direct hit, forcing its closing while the staff cleared the debris. Temporary cardboard shutters were placed over a hundred windows blown out by the blast. A few months later, the school was again closed when a parachute mine exploded nearby, further damaging the building.[6]

Educational officials at the LCC and civil servants at the Board of Education watched the effects of the war with growing concern. E.G. Savage, chief education officer at the LCC, declared in the summer of 1940 that the educational system of the country had been substantially disrupted: 'if we are not careful', he warned, 'the whole fabric will go completely to pieces'.[7] R.S. Wood, deputy secretary at the Board of Education, agreed. In a memo written in November, 1940, he declared that elementary education in London was 'not far from collapse'.[8]

No doubt some of the ill effects of the war upon education were unavoidable. But to many critics, the government's wartime educational policy seemed merely a continuation of a negligent pre-war program. In the 1920's and 1930's, conservative governments, especially, had curtailed public spending on education. Free places in grammar schools were reduced. The school leaving age remained fixed instead of raised as advocated by educational reformers. And now, under the pressures of war and evacuation, the entire system of education seemed at risk.

Would education after the war continue to be slighted? Statements by government officials were not encouraging. Herwald Ramsbotham, the Conservative President of the Board of Education, in speaking to the Incorporated Association of Assistant Masters in January, 1941, gave assurances that schools and schooling were progressing well under evacuation conditions. This was a statement difficult to credit. Reflecting the current mood among educational reformers, the _Times Educational Supplement_ found Ramsbotham's speech 'profoundly unsatisfactory'.[9] From this time forward, pressure grew for a more specific government policy on post-war education.

Among the first in recognizing the need for a comprehensive post-war reform were civil servants and educational administrators of both the LCC and the Board of Education. Their experiences in the early months of the evacuation made them exceptionally conscious of their weak administrative position. This was especially true of the Board of Education. Traditionally, the Board could only persuade or arbitrate: it had no powers of coercion over local educational authorities. The Board's structural weakness had for long contributed to its lack of prestige among the various governmental ministries. Even R.A. Butler, probably the most effective President the Board ever had, complained that other ministers did not consult him on important matters. 'I do not know why there is a Board of Education', he once upbraided his colleagues. 'Everyone tramples on it'.[10]

The Presidency of the Board of Education was perhaps the least sought of ministerial offices: able and ambitious politicians went elsewhere. Thus, the Board had difficulty in advancing educational issues to the front rank of cabinet concerns. Wartime conditions lessened the importance of the Board even further in the eyes of the Cabinet, especially after Churchill's assumption of office in May, 1940: his lack of interest in educational matters was well known. Butler believed that Churchill saw the Board essentially 'as a place where one smacked children's bottoms and blew their noses'.[11]

The war, however, imperceptibly altered the Board's authority. When local officials acted timidly or unfairly against evacuated schools, the Board could not easily bring them into line, as we have seen. Yet the Board was involved more fully in administrative problems and educational issues than in pre-war years. The problems of maintaining an educational system doubly disrupted by war and the evacuation brought about a necessary growth in the Board's authority. As the *Times Educational Supplement* astutely observed in the early days of the war, from 'the traditional idea that the business of the Board is to advise and watch', it was suddenly called upon 'to plan, control, advise'.[12]

Easing of day-to-day administrative pressures by late 1940 and removal of its staff to Bournemouth gave the Board a chance for reflection on its recent experiences.[13] The general sense among Board members was that temporary responsibilities thrust upon the Board by the evacuation should not be lost, and that future planning should incorporate the notion of the Board's newly found sense of purpose. In a memo on 'Post-War Educational Reconstruction', Sir Maurice Holmes wrote: 'I find that some of my colleagues, besides myself, have been considering whether we should not, now that we are working without constant interruptions, be bending our minds to a study of the educational problems which will arise when the war is over'. It was a matter, Holmes believed, on which the Board 'should lead rather than follow'.[14] The Board had already, in early 1940, begun to plan beyond the war years by forming a committee of senior officials who gathered ideas from various department heads on post-war reform.[15]

The growing impetus among Board members for a more active Board of Education in the post-war world was complemented by a similar growth of opinion among the main body of teachers in the state schools. They bore, as we have noted, the main brunt of the evacuation. They had little time or opportunity to institute reforms or to carry out innovative teaching; but it was obvious to them that reform--should it come--must be legislated from the top. Teachers agreed with civil servants at the Board of Education that greater powers had to be assigned to the Board. Indeed, in their view, it was necessary that the Board be elevated to a fully fledged Ministry of Education. Only a cabinet ranked ministry could create a rejuvenated national system of education. This was the theme of Ronald Gould's presidential address to the National Union of Teachers in 1943. Teachers were opposed to local options and permissive legislation in education, he claimed: they wanted local education authorities 'to be given duties, not powers'.[16]

Once the premise of a more centralized and directed national system of education had been admitted, it followed that all school children should be brought together in sharing its benefits. In other words, reform of education would naturally lead to a greater extension of education; or, as many reformers put it, to a democratization of education. This was not a new idea, but it became a potent and popular idea as the conditions of wartime Britain disproved the earlier view among evacuation planners that certain elements of the population would break in the face of enemy air attack. However unnerving the bombardments were, there was no mass panic. Indeed, as the war progressed, incidents multiplied of civilian steadiness under fire. Hard work, loyalty, and efficiency were more in evidence than fear, irresponsibility, and irresolution. Soon after the heavy bombing during the London blitz, a deputy assistant police commissioner 'off my own bat' (as he put it) surveyed Poplar, Stepney, and West Ham. He informed Sir Philip Game, the Metropolitan Police Commissioner, that, in spite of heavy casualties, morale was high.[17] In a speech before London MPs in February 1941, Sir Ernest Gowers, head of London's civil defense, confessed he had feared that the population would crack under intensive bombing. That fear had been proven wrong: 'the steadfastness of the people has been superb', he assured his listeners.[18]

Even during the V2 attacks in 1944, the population held up well, especially among children in the cities. One psychologist surveyed 7000 Bristol children after several severe air raids and found only four percent showed signs of strain.[19] The sights and sounds of air raids could even be a thrilling event to older children. A series of LCC school inspectors' reports in June, 1944, offer the most conclusive evidence of children's steadiness when under attack.[20] In Battersea and Wandsworth, the divisional inspector reported that children 'do not seem much affected' by the bombing; indeed, 'on the whole they are excited by it'. In Bermondsey, Camberwell, Deptford, Lambeth, and Southwark, the inspector observed high morale. From Greenwich, Lewisham, and Woolwich came a report of severe destruction: sixty of 112 schools had been damaged. Yet morale remained high. In Bethnal Green, the City, Popular, and Stepney, teachers reportedly were tired from lack of sleep, but morale in the schools generally was 'quite good'. In Hackney, the children in school were 'happy and contented, and in general show no sign of strain'. The Divisional Officer for Finsbury, Islington, and Holborn reported morale 'excellent' and the children 'calm and unflustered'.

Perhaps only one incident during the war can be attributed to panic--the Bethnal Green Tube disaster of 3 March 1943 when 173 men, women, and children were suffocated during a rush for shelter; but even here, there were special and unusual circumstances as the official report makes clear.[21] Nearly 2000 people were already in the shelter when the noise of an anti-aircraft battery nearby sent hundreds more to safety. The approach to the tube's lower level was down a steep and badly lit flight of steps to a landing from which another flight of stairs at a right angle descended further. Near the bottom, a woman carrying a bundle and a baby fell. Others fell on top of her and soon there was a pile-up six deep.

The steadiness of the population in the face of war was taken by James Chuter Ede, Labour member for South Shields, as a lesson for post war reform. Chuter Ede, who was also parliamentary secretary to the Board of Education, made an important speech in January, 1941, outlining the basis for reform. The battle of Dunkirk, Ede declared, had proven, if proof were needed, 'the essential soundness and toughness of British democracy'. Dunkirk had not been the achievement of a single class, but of a whole nation. Because Dunkirk had been a national effort, so, too, must be any educational reform. English education for too long had been stratified into social grades, thus perpetuating narrow class perspectives. It ought to be the goal of the Board of Education to promote reforms which would share out the privileges of the few to the many.[23]

Chuter Ede's remarks contrasted with Ramsbotham's speech a few weeks previously which the Times Educational Supplement had found so unsatisfactory. Within a few months, however, Ramsbotham had come round to Chuter Ede's point of view. In a speech to the London branch of the National Union of Teachers in May, 1941, Ramsbotham promised that forthcoming educational reforms 'would be more than mere developments within the existing framework' and would offer 'an equality of opportunity really consonant with the ideas of our democratic society'.[24]

That Ramsbotham should give official (and conservative) sanction to 'equality of opportunity' was an important step forward. It directed the focus of educational reform away from the highly selective and class oriented education which had always characterized the British system. In the past, non-fee paying elementary schools were attended mainly by working class children who prepared for a manual vocation. Fee-paying secondary schools, who received their pupils at the age of eleven, recruited from the middle classes and prepared for professional or clerical occupations. Although working class children could enter the secondary system through a free place mechanism, these were effectively limited by the constraints and needs of working class families; the loss of wages, for example, of a working class child who entered a secondary school might not be easily sustained.[25]

When Ede and like-minded reformers spoke of democratizing education, they had in mind some means of providing secondary education for all. This had been a demand of the Labour Party for two decades. But it was not a leftist slogan only. As early as 1915, the Times Educational Supplement had advocated it on purely pedagogical grounds.

Between the wars a few progressive local authorities took matters into their own hands and established 'Higher Tops' in elementary schools for able children who could not advance into secondary schools.[26] Their action reflected the growing demand for greater educational opportunities during the inter-war period among the working class. Even in unskilled working class families, there was a strong demand for better access to secondary schooling, clearly belying the assumption in some quarters that only middle-class families strove to get ahead. Most of the demand among working class families for better education, however, came from the so-called aristocracy of labour--artisans, foremen, and others hoping to make the leap into middle-class respectability.[27] These eager and entrepreneurial members of the working class were not interested in curriculum reform. For them, educational reform simply meant access to the existing educational structure so that they could advance upward through the existing class structure. Educational reform was thus for them, strictly speaking, not an educational issue, but a sociological one. The shambles of the evacuation, by retarding advances toward a broader secondary school movement, effectively blocked their upward social mobility.

Not only among the working class was there an interest in educational reform: the aspiring lower middle-class were similarly inclined. Small shopkeepers, clerks, school teachers, and distributive workers were traditionally upwardly mobile, perched as they were on the rim of full middle class respectability.[28] Perhaps more than any other part of the electorate, they were acutely conscious of the value of education as an instrument in achieving their social aims. Even more than some elements of the working class, lower-middle class aspirants heartily supported a free and well-organized educational system. The disruptions of the evacuation gave them a horror of further educational chaos.

As educational reformers--civil servants, educators, members of the Labor Party, and perhaps most importantly, working class parents--marched under the banner of secondary education for all, they drew nearer the bastion of privileged secondary education symbolized by the public schools. Throughout 1942 and 1943, the debate on the role of the public schools became the most controversial issue in educational reform. Defenders of the public schools argued for the status quo. Critics advocated their outright abolition. Still others saw some good in them and believed their educational advantages could be shared out more widely. Should there be a few Etons? None? Or a thousand?

The debate over the public schools was given prominence in February, 1942, when a young historian, A.L. Rowse, suggested in a letter to The Times that state schools ought not emulate public schools but develop their own ethos. Rowse thought it unlikely that working class parents were prepared to have their children 'taken away to be educated into a different social stratum'.[25] Defenders of public schools agreed. They hoped to retain the predominant social composition as it then was--upper- and middle-class with only a leavening of bright working class boys. A large influx of working class children would inevitably alter public schools, perhaps even forcing out the boarding school principle, substituting for it day schooling. Public schools believed that their advantages--especially the development of character and a religious view of life--were direct consequences of communal living and an enforced corporate structure.

There was a complementary danger if admissions to public schools from among the disadvantaged increased as a consequence of the abolition of tuition fees. The character of the nation's children could be undermined because, as the Headmaster of Harrow put it, 'a bad view of the State as the universal provider' would go abroad in the country.[30]

It was in the nature of the controversy that loyal old boys carried their defence of the public schools too far. One correspondent to The Times declared that public schools spoiled far fewer children than 'incompetent parents'.[31] Even less sensitive to many wartime Britons was the assertion of the president of the Incorporated Association of Headmasters that the Battle of Britain had been 'fought largely by our old boys, for few apart from them had the education and training necessary to become air crews'.[32] Perhaps most damning to the cause of public schools was a speech made by Sir Cyril Norwood at Tonbridge School in late 1943. Admitting that public schools were privileged, Sir Cyril, a former headmaster of Harrow, believed a liquidation of public schools was 'beyond common sense' because 'the nation needed character, brains, and industry' and 'we could not afford to level down'.[33]

More moderate defenders of the public schools, especially those who were Conservative members of the coalition government, attempted to blur the rougher edges of the controversy. Lord Chancellor Simon, in a speech at Repton School, drew on the experiences of the evacuation in suggesting not the elimination of public schools, but rather an extension of their benefits. The establishment of hostels for evacuees and the incorporation of some evacuated schools into what were virtually boarding schools, he argued, 'had shown that life in a special community might benefit children of all classes from the standpoint of the development of character as well as of physical and mental improvement'.[34]

Not everyone drew Lord Simon's lesson and the association of the public schools with the evacuation was galling to many. Evacuated teachers and students had little sense that they were part of a privileged educational group. And it seemed that the evacuated public schools retained their privileges even when evacuated. Pictures in the newspaper press of Malvern College, splendidly housed at Blenheim, did not go unnoticed. In the main, it appears that public schools weathered the evacuation with their students and staff intact: they could rely upon an extensive and influential network to overcome their most severe difficulties.[35]

By the middle years of the war, the educational reform movement was gathering strength, fuelled in part by the failures of the evacuation. As educational reform merged into the broader democratic movement, the tide against privileged education rose ever higher. Spokesmen organized with increasing effect. As may be expected, trade unions, organs of the Labour

Party, and educational officials were especially active. The Trades Union Congress believed unequivocally that public schools ought to be a part of a national system of education. Charles Dukes, general secretary of the National Union of General and Municipal Workers, declared in 1942 his union's demand of 'one uniform education for everyone'.[36] The National Union of Teachers held similar views. Its president, in calling for educational unity in 1942, condemned the public school which 'embodied and organized within the nation a privileged class'.[37] The Labour dominated London County Council also took a strong stand against public schools. The LCC advocated free secondary education for all children, promoted day schooling over boarding schools, and recommended the abolition of schools run for private profit. Lord Latham, a Labour peer and leader of the LCC, declared that public schools had 'no place of privilege in the educational world of tomorrow'.[38] T.H. Jones, chairman of the LCC Educational Sub-Committee, put it in more homely terms: whereas public schools wanted themselves to be 'as public as the Ritz, ...we want them to be as public as the pub around the corner'.[39]

Most critical of the public schools was the Workers' Educational Association, led by its president, R.H. Tawney, long an advocate of the abolition of privileged education. Indeed, Tawney and the WEA opposed private preparatory schools as well as the secondary level public schools. Tawney declared bluntly: 'the country was heartily sick of distinctions between schools based on differences in wealth and social status'.[40] For Tawney and others who thought like him, the very existence of public schools within a reconstructed postwar society would be an anomaly. As the socialist <u>New Statesman</u> summed it up: 'A truly democratic educational system inside a plutocracy is a contradiction in terms'.[41]

Outside labour and the unions, the <u>Times Educational Supplement</u> made the strongest case for education playing a role in the needs of a more democratic postwar society. In a series of leading articles beginning in the latter months of 1942, the <u>TES</u> placed itself in the forefront of educational reconstruction. Too many educational reformers in the past, the _TES_ claimed, had spent their energies 'in seeking to prop up, extend, and elaborate what is admittedly a derelict building'. Educational changes may necessarily become 'revolutionary' if Britain were to have an educational system 'adequate to act as an effective instrument for the creation of a fully democratic society'.[42] Even _The Times_ admitted the weakness of the public school system. As 'an instrument of social privilege', it had conferred on its beneficiaries 'something like a monopoly of the leading positions in politics, public administration, and, latterly, business'.[43]

Public school officials were not indifferent to the rising tide of criticism. The more responsible among them were willing to come to terms with the reform movement in large part because of public schools' weakened financial position. Erosion had begun in the depression of the 1930s and had been exacerbated during the war. Parents could no longer pay the fees. Thus a basis for some kind of accommodation existed. The public schools would be willing to accept a larger role of the state in their affairs through inspection and a closer integration of public schools within a national system of education. In return, the public schools would open their doors to more pupils subsidized by the state. The first tentative probing between the public schools and government officials began before the war. At the time of the Munich crisis, Sir Maurice Holmes, at the Board of Education, wrote to the headmaster of Winchester suggesting discussions on matters of common interest; but, Holmes cautioned, the discussions should be initiated by the public schools themselves, preferably by the Headmasters' Conference lest it appear that the civil service was promoting favoritism. Holmes, himself a graduate of Wellington and Oxford, and a governor of Wellington at the time, feared that war, should it break out, would mean an educational disruption great enough to bring down the weaker public schools. Some special means of compensation, he believed, could be devised.[44] Thoughts similar to Holmes' were in the minds of interested parties outside the civil service. At the time that Holmes was beginning his initiative, he received a letter from Sir Cyril Norwood suggesting a government commission to investigate grounds of cooperation between the state and the public schools.[45]

Clearly, a salvage operation was forming, encouraged and perhaps led by ex-public school boys within the civil service. It would seem an obvious case of a conflict of interest: members of an ostensibly disinterested bureaucracy pledged to uphold the national system of education were maneuvering with the representatives of a privileged system of education for the benefit of the privileged. It also suggests a secret alliance in the heart of the government machinery which could effectively block a complete democratization of the school system. It attests, in short, to class privilege perpetuated through the public school system--the very point made by the most severe critics of the public schools.

It fell upon R.A. Butler, who succeeded Ramsbotham at the Board of Education in 1941, to settle the public school controversy within the broader context of educational reconstruction. In reconciling the conflicting parties, Butler brought considerable political gifts. He also brought a willingness to consult widely with all the concerned parties, and an ability to establish essential compromises. A speech before the annual meeting of the Association of Education Committees in 1942 suggested his strategy. He claimed that education would be the spearhead of post-war social reform--a progressive, even radical statement. But this was balanced by a more cautious aim in the same speech: he declared his respect for a diversity of schools within the educational system while simultaneously eliminating their diversity of standards.[46] In fact, Butler's ultimate loyalty lay with the public schools. As he confided to a Glasgow Unionist Association in 1943, 'education should not be chained to the chariot of the state....boys and girls should not be brought up on one mould or pattern'.[47] More indicative of Butler's sympathies was a letter to the Bishop of London in late 1941. 'I hope', Butler wrote, 'I may take it that our talk can be absolutely private since there is such a big avalanche which will be let loose on the subject of the public schools. If we do not meet unofficially we cannot talk to the benefit of those institutions which you are doing so much to help'.[48]

Such a powerful alliance was bound to have good effect for the public schools. A legislative benefit came early in the war. The passage of the Public and Other Schools (War Conditions) Act of 1941 enabled schools with endowments to apply the income or capital for purposes other than those for which it was originally intended. In the following year, the government appointed the Fleming Committee ostensibly to investigate ways of increasing cooperation between public schools and the national system. As Gosden has pointed out, it was thought at the time that the Committee's specific charge was to explore the possibilities of reconstructing education by extending the advantages of public schools to the national system. But it also seems the Committee hoped to find ways of bringing state support to endangered public schools. In addition, Butler used the Committee as a device to divert the public schools controversy away from the larger issue of educational reconstruction.[49] Butler had already decided that the public schools should remain largely untouched by postwar reform. Part of his reasoning was based on the need to comply with a directive from Churchill, which instructed Butler not 'to stir up the public schools question'.[50] In allowing the Fleming Committee to hold the ring of the public schools controversy, Butler could go forward with his reform program, and once it had passed into law, the topic of the public schools would be less controversial. In short, by giving the educational reformers most of what they wanted, Butler could retain the public schools largely intact.

Butler's strategy was wholly successful. The Education Act of 1944 has been hailed as a milestone for education. The Act was widely praised in its day as a progressive and comprehensive measure, even among many in the Labour Party. But it did not substantially touch the public schools. Nor did it change the notion of a three-tiered state educational system which had grown up during the interwar period--secondary modern schools for the great mass of students; technical schools for those interested in applied science or applied art; and grammar schools for the brightest few. The idea of segregating children according to innate ability and intelligence had been given formal status by the Spens Report of 1938 and the Hadow Report of 1943. These reports represented the prevailing view among educational administrators of the time; they, in turn, had been largely influenced by the ideas of Cyril Burt.[51] That children could be relegated to specific schools suitable to their likely life careers was widely held, not only among educators and psychologists.

When the implications of the Act of 1944 were discussed by the Hampshire County Council, one Councillor explained to his colleagues that under the act, a child's 'ability and learning for its calling in life would be decided' at the age of eleven. Most children would be sent to secondary modern schools because 'the average of the human brain was not too high'.[52] Butler himself seems to have held this view, or so claimed one of the few groups to oppose the Act of 1944, the National Association of Labour Teachers, a left-wing ginger group of the National Union of Teachers. NALT advocated a national system of multilateral schools where all classes of pupils would be brought together to receive the benefits of a common educational experience. One NALT member charged that Butler was a 'neo-platonist' who saw inflexible gradations of ability and intelligence among school children.[53] It has also been charged that the 'reactionary' civil servants under the Board of Education were unsympathetic to a thorough-going reform and believed implicitly in the hierarchical system of traditional education.[54] One need not go so far as this to understand that civil servants would be naturally eager to protect the school system of which they had been a part. It certainly seems true that the civil service acted as a moderating force upon post-war Labour Ministers of Education.[55]

The most notable provision of the 1944 Act was the creation of a strong central authority to regulate education. This provision especially pleased educational reformers. It also appealed to some conservatives who were convinced by the events of the war that centralization was justified. The Times, in commending the Act, declared that centralization was necessary in the case of education on the grounds of efficiency and equality of opportunity: 'no system can consist of isolated or irresponsible units. These must be welded together, and given a sense of common purpose and direction'.[56]

These remarks, coming from an influential source and doubtless reflecting a large body of opinion, could as easily be applied to the reconstruction of society as a whole. It could be argued that efficiency and equality of opportunity were desirable ends in themselves: they need not be hitched to a socialist wagon to justify the strengthening of central authority in other areas of life. Therefore the leftward swing during the war about which much has been written need not be seen as inevitably traceable to a rise in socialist sympathies. The electorate, including many Labour supporters, were probably not so much interested in the nationalization of industry, or in centralization as a matter of principle, as they were in assuring that the postwar world would go well for them. They wanted a more assured access to those institutions which allowed them to rise higher in society. Thus their interest in educational reform.

The irony of the Educational Act of 1944, of course, was that it was brought about by a conservative minister in a Conservative-dominated coalition government, whose Conservative chief was uninterested in educational policy. In a sense, the Act--incomplete as it was--gave a taste of reform to the country at large. It was the first of the great movements of reconstruction that shaped to the post-war world in Britain. A double irony inherent in its passage was that the Conservative political establishment thought it would be a harmless diversion away from more serious issues. The Conservative whips believed, as Butler noted, that the bill 'provided endless opportunity for debate on issues which in their view were not vital to the war and which would keep Members thoroughly occupied without breaking up the Government'.[57] This was a view that naturally commended itself to Churchill.

This somewhat cynical attitude toward educational reform among Conservatives gave an advantage to the Labour Party. Though the

Conservatives may have passed the bill, would they energetically carry it through? Public suspicion of Conservative intentions had arisen because of the educational chaos of the evacuation, and the pre-war record of conservative governments. In addition, a series of reports on post-war educational reconstruction issued by the Conservative Sub-Committee on Education had been poorly received. The social and political philosophy of the Conservatives had been strongly woven into the fabric of the reports: the tone alarmed many, especially its stress on religious education; the role of education in inculcating patriotism; and the Conservative concern for public order after the war, especially in the juvenile population, for whom compulsive leisure time activities were prescribed.[58]

The Labour Party played upon the public's unease of Conservative intentions. As we have seen, Labourites had established themselves as early and severe critics of the Board of Education's actions during the evacuation. Labour kept up its attacks on educational policy throughout the war in a series of pamphlets and books. At the height of the evacuation controversy, Transport House, Labour Party headquarters, published Susan Lawrence's _The Children's Welfare in War Time_ (1940) which set out in print many of the criticisms made by the Parliamentary Labour Party during debates in the House of Commons. Lawrence declared that the first casualty of the war had been the system of universal compulsory education carefully built up over many years. 'We have indeed to go back to the eighteen seventies', she wrote, 'to find anything like the present state of affairs in some of our great cities'. The blame could be laid squarely at the door of the 'idle and apathetic' Board of Education, a Board whose record was merely a reflection of the pre-war Conservative educational policy. Essential to education was a Board which could offer 'drive and vision'. Other publications sponsored by the Labour Party argued that educational difficulties in war-time had deep roots. Ernest Green's _Education in a New Society_ (1942), published by the Labour Book Service, explained how educational inequities could be traced to the wide diversity of practices among local educational authorities. Under some authorities, rates were high: in others, low. The benefits to education would vary accordingly. And the difference between state schools and public schools was even greater. Green noted that on the children of Boston in Lincolnshire, slightly more than nine pounds were expended annually, whereas Eton spent 315 pounds on each pupil.

Thus Labour co-opted the Educational Act by simultaneously criticizing the Conservative record in education and pointing out the most progressive aspects of the Act as their own. Labour could play on the fears of those who believed a post-war Conservative government would be slow in implementing the Act. The suspicion that the Conservatives as a whole were not enthusiastic for the Act was strengthened by their diffidence in receiving the Beveridge Report, a diffidence based in part on narrow Treasury grounds. There was also a feeling among Conservatives, as Butler reported, that Beveridge was 'a sinister old man, who wishes to give away a great deal of other people's money'.[59] This had too familiar a ring for those who remembered the restrictive conservative educational budgets of the 1920s and 1930s. The Labour Party benefitted. It was widely believed that Labour would fully implement the Act of 1944. Labour as a party of order and action was, indeed, the image put forth by the party during the 1945 campaign. 'Let Us Face the Future', the Party's now famous election manifesto, emphasized that Labour stood for order against chaos, and for purposive constructive progress against 'do-as-they please anarchy'--in educational reconstruction as in all else.

NOTES

1. First hand information about individual schools may be found in school log books. A large collection is in the Greater London Record Office. Those cited here include: D.O. 1, Langford Road 'I' 1933-1950; D.O. 1 Peterborough 'M' 1940-1946; D.O. 5 Devons Road Emergency 'J.M'. 1942-1947.

2. GLRO EO/WAR/3/14.

3. Information on the Sandhurst Road School disaster may be found in the Divisional Officer's report to the LCC, GLRO EO/WAR/3/28, 21 January 1943.

4. PRO ED 138/35.

5. P.H.J.H. Gosden, *How They Were Taught* (New York, 1969), pp. 245-46.

6. For information on Bristol's evacuation and wartime schooling, see C.M. MacInnes, *Bristol at War* (London, 1962); Bristol Record Office, Evacuation Committee Minute Book, 1940-1945; and Bristol Record Office, School Logbooks.

7. PRO ED 134/77, 16 July 1940.

8. PRO ED 136/665, 4 November 1940.

9. *TES*, 4 January 1941.

10. British Library, Chuter-Ede Diary, Add Mss 59691, 16 October 1941.

11. Lord Butler, *The Art of Memory* (London, 1982), p. 152.

12. *TES*, 25 November 1939.

13. Ministry of Education, *Education, 1900-1950* (London, HMSO, 1951), Cmd 8244.

14. PRO ED 136/212.

15. Gosden, *Education in the Second World War*, Ch. 11; R.G. Wallace, 'The Origins and Authorship of the 1944 Education Act', *History of Education*, vol. 10, no. 4 (1981), pp. 283-290.

16. *The Times*, 29 April 1943.

17. PRO HO 186/342.

18. Hodsoll Papers 5/12 (Churchill College, Cambridge).

19. Frank Bodman, 'Child Psychiatry in War Time Britain', *Journal of Educational Psychology*, vol. XXXV, no. 5 (May 1944), pp. 293-301.

20. GLRO EO/WAR/3/18.

21. *Report...into the Accident at Bethnal Green Tube Station Shelter* (London, HMSO, 1943), Cmd 6583.

22. See, for example, Bodman, 'Child Psychiatry in War Time Britain', *Journal of Educational Psychology*; Rosemary Pritchard and Saul Rosenzweig, 'The Effects of War Stress upon Childhood and Youth', *The Journal of Abnormal and Social Psychology*, vol. 37, no. 3 (July 1942), pp. 329-344; and P.E. Vernon, 'Psychological Effects of Air-Raids', *Journal of Abnormal and Social Psychology*, vol. 36, no. 4 (October 1941), pp. 457-476.

23. *The Times*, 28 January 1941.

24. *Ibid*., 13 May 1941.

25. Michael Parkinson, *The Labour Party and the Organization of Education, 1918-1965* (London, 1970).

26. Olive Banks, *Parity and Prestige in English Secondary Education* (London, 1955).

27. J.E. Floud *et. al*., *Social Class and Educational Opportunity* (London, 1957); Thomas W. Laqueur, 'Working Class Demand and the Growth of English Elementary Education, 1750-1850', in Lawrence Stone (ed.), *Schooling and Society: Studies in the History of Education* (Baltimore, 1976), pp. 192-205; and C.M. Turner, 'Sociological Approaches to the History of Education', *British Journal of Educational Studies*, vol. XVII, no. 2 (June 1969), pp. 146-165.

28. Geoffrey Crossick, 'The Emergence of the Lower Middle Class in Britain: A Discussion', in Geoffrey Crossick (ed.), *The Lower Middle Class in Britain, 1870-1914* (New York, 1977).

29. *The Times*, 27 February 1942.

30. *Ibid*., 21 January 1943.

31. *Ibid*., 17 July 1942.

32. *Ibid*., 6 January 1943.

33. *TES*, 6 November 1943.

34. *The Times*, 26 June 1943.

35. See, for example, H.C.A. Gaunt, *Two Exiles: Being a Record of Malvern College during the War* (London, 1946); J.C.H.T., *Clifton at Bude and Butcombe: The Story of a School in Evacuation* (Bristol, 1945). For an example of a private preparatory school, see J.H. Leakey, *School Errant: The Story of the War-Time Adventures of Dulwich College Preparatory School* (London, 1951).

36. *The Times*, 9 June 1942.

37. *Ibid*., 9 April 1942.

38. *Ibid*., 28 January 1943.

39. *Ibid*., 23 January 1943.

40. *Ibid*., 23 January 1942.

41. *New Statesman*, 4 July 1942.

42. *TES*, 31 October 1942.

43. *The Times*, 17 March 1942.

44. The discussion that follows owes much to Gosden, *Education in the Second World War*, pp. 333-339.

45. Brian Simon, *The Politics of Educational Reform* (London, 1974).

46. *The Times*, 12 June 1942.

47. *Ibid*., 23 February 1943.

48. PRO ED 136/129, 4 October 1941; cited in Gosden, *Education in the Second World War*, p. 339. The Bishop, Geoffrey Fisher, was a graduate of Marlborough and Oxford, and was once headmaster at Repton.

49. As reported by Butler's most recent biographer, Patrick Cosgrave, *R. A. Bulter: An*

English Life (London, 1981), pp. 71 and 79.

50. Lord Butler, *The Art of the Possible* (Penguin Books, 1975), p. 95.

51. See I.G.K. Fenwick, *The Comprehensive School, 1944-1970: The Politics of Secondary School Reorganization* (London, 1976), chs. 1-3; and Stephen Jay Gould, *The Mismeasure of Man* (New York, 1981), ch. 6.

52. Hampshire Record Office, Hampshire County Council Minutes, 16 November 1944.

53. Jules David Burgevin, 'Politics and Education: Case Study of a Pressure Group, the National Association of Labour Teachers, 1927-1951' (Syracuse University Ph.D. Dissertation, 1969) p. 128.

54. David Rubinstein, 'Ellen Wilkinson Re-considered', *History Workshop*, vol. 7 (Spring, 1979), pp. 161-169.

55. Betty D. Vernon, *Ellen Wilkinson, 1891-1947* (London, 1982).

56. *The Times*, 19 January 1944.

57. R.A. Butler Papers, Trinity College, Cambridge, G15, 172.

58. D.W. Dean, 'Problems of the Conservative Sub-committee on Education, 1941-45', *Journal of Educational Administration and History*, vol. III, no. 1 (December 1970), pp. 26-37.

59. Butler Papers, G15,91.

CHAPTER VIII

The Evacuation and Post-War Britain

Thus far, we have discussed the evacuation in its social aspects; that is, how it may have affected the perceptions and images of evacuees and their rural hosts. We have noted in many instances that class and ethnic prejudices were as common as a spirit of war-time camaraderie. We have seen the clash between central authority and local officials over the administration of the evacuation. And we have observed that chaotic conditions in education raised concerns about the future of education in the post-war world. In this chapter, we discuss how these issues helped shape a political climate favorable to the Labour Party and how this political climate helps explain the astonishing Labour victory in 1945. We also examine how the evacuation may have prepared the electorate for the sweeping social legislation which followed the Labour victory.

It must first be admitted that the argument advanced here is speculative. We are attempting to derive political meaning from the evacuation across a very wide spectrum of evacuation experiences. These generalizations can only be verified by local studies. The first difficulty in establishing the truth of our argument lies, in short, in the very scope of the evacuation itself. The second major difficulty lies in the lack of specific evidence as it relates to the election of 1945. Election studies were in their infancy at the end of the war, and the justly famous Nuffield Election series, whose first volume began in 1945, provides only a rough guide to the election. Studies since then have not been much more helpful, an extraordinary state of affairs given the importance of that election to the shape of post-war politics. Explanations about Labour's victory tend toward the general: for example, Kenneth Brown's belief that the electorate in 1945 was determined 'to have done with the old and to look to the future'; or Henry Pelling's observation that the electorate was fearful of a return to the pre-war depression.[1] No doubt there is something to these observations, and they would seem to make good sense; but they lack a grounding in specific grievances and discrete groups of the population. Was everyone finished with the old? Why should the future hold a better promise in a wartorn and chaotic world? Years of depression and war would seem as likely to make one fearful of the future.

Our argument in this chapter is that the evacuation, because it uprooted significant numbers of urban poor beyond their traditional boundaries forced social comparisons between them and their more affluent rural countrymen. Thus, the evacuation revealed to many of the urban poor--a natural Labour constituency--the realities of class and privilege in Britain. The process of social comparison engendered by the evacuation was not only a living demonstration of upper class wealth; but it led to a heightened sense of class awareness among many urban dwellers. By thus making cohesive their common lot and aspirations, the evacuation provided a spur to their concerted action to attain common goals.

It may seem at first blush that the working class knew well enough the disadvantages of the class system. Undoubtedly this was true among the more politically conscious working class spokesmen. Many workers, however, were apolitical and lived out their lives in isolated communities with no direct knowledge of existing social structures. To them, class and class divisions were abstractions. Typical enough was the early life of Louis Heren, who became a prominent journalist for The Times.[2] His native parish, Shadwell, lay by the Thames. Shadwellian men worked on the docks: the women often laboured as chars in the city. Heren's mother ran a coffee shop: his father, a printer, died when Heren was four. Shadwellians rarely went beyond the nearby environs, except for bank holiday fairs on Hampstead Heath, or hop gathering in Kent. Although the children sang the Internationale and the Red Flag in school and had vague socialist sympathies, they lacked firsthand knowledge of the class system. Heren confesses that he felt neither poor nor deprived when growing up.[3] Not until he went to Sandhurst as an officer cadet in World War II did he become aware of the British class system. Heren's experiences with the wider world beyond his working class parish can be multiplied many times among the evacuees. Robert Roberts, in his description of slum life in Salford, reports a similar story of loosely structured self-contained urban villages in which each family had a recognized place in the community. Insofar as there was a class struggle, it was apolitical. Economic struggles that ensued were not against exploitive employers, but lonely, isolated battles for survival.[4] A similar theme emerges from Madeline Kerr's study of the pseudononymous Ship Street, a Liverpool slum. Fifty out of the sixty-one families examined had lived in the neighbourhood all their lives.[5]

Whether or not working class Britains are, or ought to be, 'class conscious' has generated a considerable body of literature. Generally speaking, the traditional Marxist view would have it that manual workers of the type that provided the core of the evacuee experience were the heart of any proletarian revolutionary movement. This idea has been considerably modified over time; and, in fact, the more closely one examines manual workers, the less easy it is to generalize about their social or political beliefs. Frank Parkin has even inverted Marxism and held that workers tend to be natural conservatives because they often identify with the established institutions of British society, which are essentially conservative in nature, such as the monarchy, the Church, and the idea of a reasoned dissent embodied in the parliamentary system.[6]

What seems to be most important to the workers in their political behavior is how they viewed themselves within the class structure. Here the evidence seems substantially in agreement.[7] If a docker saw himself as a member of the working class, he would likely vote Labour:

but if he saw himself as a member of the lower middle class, he would more likely vote Conservative. In part, such a voter would express his aspirations for a higher class ranking; and in part the voter would reject his background.

How could the evacuation experienoc of working class Britains have caused an abnormally large number of them to embrace their working class position, and to reject the notion of a more desirable middle class position? From our discussion in the chapters above, it is obvious that the rejection came in the initial instance at the hands of the middle class. Those affluent rural hosts who were expected to welcome working class evacuees instead thrust them from their homes. The shock of rejection, later enlivened by other wartime grievances, politicized working class families strongly enough to draw them into an uncharacteristically active political behavior.

One may imagine easily enough the enclosed working class communities in shipbuilding or docking areas of large urban centers, or even in the more diverse occupational sections of urban slums as they discussed the conduct of the war and of the civilian evacuation. Working class women in their densely packed streets kept stories and rumours flying. Working class men in their pubs and on the job kept pace with the latest tale of middle-class irresponsibility and heartlessness. They had trusted and believed in the Conservative government to lead their wives and children to safety: it was a trust betrayed.

As the evacuation scheme collapsed in the early months of the war, a sense of grievance crystallized into a determination to do something about the problem. Political activism was the obvious response. That working class Britons were drawn more actively into political life is born out by some circumstantial evidence. For example, a study of local constituency politics in Newcastle-under-Lyme notes for the first time in the city's history the development of a genuine mass Labour party during the war.[8] The greatest increase in its membership came from the working class and the lower middle class. Manual workers expecially became active. If this single example were valid for the country as a whole, it suggests that an engaged working class interest in politics promoted a larger Labour turnout in 1945 than in previous elections. A recent study by Roger Eatwell believes this to be the case. Eatwell postulates that Labour's victory was essentially a working class one largely due to the growth of a sense of their own identity, and of their determination to elect a government representative of their aims and aspirations. Eatwell's evidence is drawn in part from Mass Observation surveys which found that the main reason workers voted Labour was their identification as a working class: 43% gave it as their reason, far ahead of the next reason given, a desire for nationalization, at only 6%.[9]

Of course, it is important not to over-emphasize the evacuation to the exclusion of the other unsettling events of the war which could have had similar effects upon working class Britons. Paul Addison, as we have noted, has set out the various influences for political and social reform during the war. But as Addison himself observed, the leftward shift in political opinion was significant very early in the war, perhaps as early as 1940.[10] The only event which could have had such an impact so early in the war years was the evacuation of hundreds of thousands of working class Britons.

It must seem obvious, too, that the evacuation had an impact upon post-war social planning. We have already documented the growth of the central government in post-war educational reform. The notion that the state should take a more active role in regulating the various voluntary agencies involved in social work can also be traced in part to the evacuation. One of the earliest examples of this 'trend toward planning' (as Paul Addison put it) was a report published in 1941 entitled _Evacuation and the Churches_. Based on a survey of Anglican and Free Churches in selected boroughs, the report first observed the destructive impact of the evacuation upon religious practice in the early days of the war. The evacuation had 'destroyed or seriously depleted Sunday schools and youth societies, the nurseries of the Church; subtracted workers and leaders; left dismal gaps in the pews; decimated choirs; torpedoed budgets'. [11] The report then turned its attention to voluntary societies (such as the churches, the WVS, and the Women's Institutes) involved in social welfare services. Although the voluntary groups had 'held the breach gallantly' during the evacuation, it was clear 'that the problems...involved in evacuation demanded a larger measure of State control...'.[12] Evacuation had revealed that 'the scattered attack of unrelated units is as inefficient as it is costly'.[13] The lesson of the evacuation ought to be clear to all. Some kind of state machinery was necessary 'to harmonise and reinforce the efforts of voluntary bodies in the realm of social welfare'.[14]

Doubts about the efficacy of voluntarism were also fuelled by practical problems relating directly to evacuated children. Although the government was loath to tamper with the machinery of evacuation, in some instances state intervention was crucial to the maintenance of the health and welfare of evacuees. How state intervention could help solve the social problems of the evacuation may best be illustrated in the school meals and the complementary, though separately administered, milk program.[15] Prior to the war, the provision of meals and milk to elementary school children was on a small scale. Only 110,000 or 2.4% received free meals in urban centers. In addition, the program was tainted with a poor law mentality: it was necessary to prove children both in need and undernourished before they could receive meals. Inadequate food was frequently served, often by private caterers. The feeding centers had an unwholesome reputation among children, parents, and teachers. A smaller group of rural children, about fifty thousand, had a more satisfactory meal time arrangement, with appetising food served in attractive school canteens. Generally speaking, the milk program boasted a better record, serving many more children and making less of a distinction between needy children and others.

Some of the problems in the program could be directly traced to its local administration. Local Education Authorities were responsible for finding needy children, and then contracting for the meals and milk. The Board of Education had no power of coercion: it could only encourage the

LEAs to expand the program. This was discouraging work. Of sixty-six LEAs visited just prior to the war, only 5% were found to be making satisfactory arrangements; 20% were entirely unsatisfactory. The remainder were not up to a very high standard.

The war made an immediate impact upon the meals and milk programs by dislocating children throughout the country. In October, 1939, a million fewer children received milk than before the war--a 40% decline. By March 1940 only half this number had been made up. The meals program suffered similarly. Because it would obviously be difficult to exclude local children, the Board pressed the LEAs to organize communal meals for all children in the reception areas. Providing mid-day meals for evacuee children was necessary not only on social and humanitarian grounds, but also, the Board believed, it would help unburden the rural hosts by keeping their evacuees at school all day. This was a view held in the reception areas as well. A Hertfordshire County Council sub-committee, for example, decided to establish communal feeding in the county because foster parents 'will probably eventually tire of the unrelieved responsibility of caring for the children for an indefinite period...'.[16]

In July 1940, decisive government action led to a broadening of the scope of the meals service, and to improve its quality. A national milk scheme was also adopted. No longer was the program to be left to the initiative of local authorities. But difficulties remained before these decisions could be implemented successfully. In the milk scheme, for example, there were serious shortages of milk and milk bottles; and a need to balance the profit motives of the dairy companies with the social needs of school children. Most of the problems were resolved, however, and by the end of the war, meals in schools had multiplied considerably. Whereas one child in thirty had been fed in 1940, by 1945 one child in three was fed at school. Only a small percentage of these meals were free, but at least the machinery was in place, and the price for parents who could afford to pay was nominal.

Titmuss believed that the developments in the meals and milk program during the war represented a revolution in the minds of parents, teachers, and children. In place of a disreputable and unpopular relief measure, the program had been within a short time accepted as a social service within the schools.[17] The evacuation had, in effect, prepared the way for a further extension of the notion of social responsibility by the state for its citizens.

A similar story may be found in the growth of state responsibility for nursery schools. Before World War II, only 180,000 of 1.75 million eligible children were attending a publicly sponsored nursery. When the evacuation suddenly swept thousands of young children into the countryside, the need for day nurseries was immediate and desperate. Children of nursery age--the under-fives--were among the most difficult to billet. Their natural noise and rowdiness was exacerbated for rural hosts because the children were not old enough to attend local schools. Remaining in the billets most of the day, the children drove their hosts to distraction. The necessity of relieving householders weighed heavily on evacuation authorities. In November, 1939, a joint committee of the Ministry of Health and the Board of Education recommended the Nursery Centres Scheme, a national system of nurseries which would draw the under-fives out of their billets for the best part of the day. But the Treasury thought the scheme too expensive and delayed its approval. By the time the Treasury had come round, most of the under-fives had drifted back with the school-aged children, and the need for nurseries had lessened.

During the second wave of evacuation in 1940, the primary reason for establishing nurseries shifted. From relieving householders, the government now focused on drawing women into the wartime workforce: this included mothers with young children. Thus the Nursery Centres Scheme was revived in June, 1940. At first, the scheme was confined to those areas where recognized shortages of wartime workers existed. As the Ministry of Health put it, welfare authorities were to 'make use of any reserves of female labour that existed within travelling distance of the important war factories, and in order to recruit such women without jeopardising the well-being of the children day nurseries must be speedily provided'.[18]

The Exchequer bore the full cost of the nurseries, although they were managed by local authorities. It was soon apparent, however, that local officials, already burdened by other wartime responsibilities, could not respond quickly or adequately enough. Some sort of central co-ordination was imperative. In April, 1941, the Ministry of Health was put in charge, giving new life to the wartime day nurseries movement. Within a few months, nearly two hundred nurseries were opened, another two hundred were approved, and three hundred more were in active preparation.

Residential nurseries, contrasted with the day nurseries, have a different history: traditionally they were homes for children without parents. As the numbers of orphaned and abandoned children rose dramatically during the war, the need for new residential nurseries grew proportionately. At first, the financial burden was carried by private philanthropic organizations, some of them from overseas, such as the American Red Cross. But by late 1940, following the trend elsewhere, the Treasury was covering most of the cost.

As is well known, the government sponsored nursery centres largely closed down after the war. The Exchequer's grant to local authorities was reduced by half, and the responsibility of financing and managing the nurseries was given to local authorities. This had the effect of throwing the whole matter to the idiosyncracies and individual practices of the regions, as Denise Riley has pointedly observed.[19] Some medical officers of health were opposed to nurseries on principle; whereas others were sympathetic, if inexperienced. By the end of 1947, only 879 day nurseries remained from a wartime peak of nearly 1600.

Clearly, in the case of nursery centres, the government throught in more immediate terms of war production, rather than an extension of a social service for the future. But for our purpose here, the fact of the evacuation edging the government forward in yet another, if temporary, social sphere was an important contribution to creating a climate of opinion willing to accept an extension of state machinery. Local officials had become especially conscious of the need for a central regulation of the problems brought on initially by the evacuation. Within a short time, local officials had to cope with the educational and housing problems of the evacuees; with communal feeding; providing nurseries; communal washing facilities; and occupational clubs for adult evacuees. Forced by wartime exigencies, local governments had to cope as best they could until the central government could formalize unofficial arrangements.

Another example we may cite of the influence of the evacuation upon the growth of the central government's responsibility was the establishment of sick bays. Evacuees who suffered minor ailments such as colds, fever, or digestive disturbances were sent to sick bays, often temporarily thrown up by local authorities. But the authorities did not always have sufficient resources to administer the sick bays: they were increasingly forced to call upon the resources of the central government. In Beaconsfield (Bucks), for example, a meeting of the evacuation sub-committee of the District Council wrote to the Ministry of Health to request help in establishing a sick bay after the suggestion had been put forward by the WVS.[20] Not every county council sanctioned sick bays. Shropshire, for example, decided not to administer them. Instead, the Ministry of Health authorized directly any local authority under the Shropshire County Council to establish a sick bay.[21] Thus county government was bypassed in this instance, and a direct link established between central and the lowest level of local government.

The need for government intervention to sort out the social chaos of the evacuation increased as the war drew on and other forms of evacuation disrupted settled population areas. War workers and the movement of government officials, sometimes whole departments, had to be accommodated in the countryside: these occupational evacuees often competed for billeting with the evacuee schoolchildren. As of October, 1940, for example, in and around Cirencester,

Gloucestershire, the military had requisitioned several large houses and had set aside accommodation for nearly four hundred. Nearby in Nailsworth, two factories had recently relocated from London. Elsewhere in the county, a large influx of munitions workers as well as aircraft workers had moved in. In Warmly the Bristol Aeroplane Company had taken over a large local plant. In Cheltenham, the Air Ministry requisitioned a number of buildings. Additionally, private evacuees were constantly arriving.[22]

Clearly, the serious overcrowding and haphazard movement of the Forces and the essential occupations, especially into the west and north-west, created a general scramble which only the central government could manage. In January 1941, the Ministry of Health issued a Lodging Restriction Order which prohibited householders from giving or letting lodgings unless it had been cleared with local authorities. Thus, the government could set priorities on occupational evacuees and where they should live. By the end of 1943, more than forty towns and districts had been closed entirely to all but essential war workers.[23] This represented the culmination of the idea that housing was in the public domain, and that the government had the right and duty to control even private domiciles during an emergency.

Lessons of the evacuation were easy enough for all to understand. The idea of voluntarism which had been at the heart of the evacuation planning before the war could no longer be sufficient to carry out the aims of the evacuation. Ill-defined functions between voluntary bodies and the government had now to be made explicit. A sub-committee of the Hertfordshire County Council put it straightforwardly in early 1941: 'it is obvious that on the success of the evacuation much still depends, and it is apparent that the Government are now aware that this success cannot be obtained by simply leaving people to adapt themselves to the social upheaval which has in fact taken place, but that there must be skilled advice, and facilities provided in order that evacuees and local householders may be able to bear the strain'.[24]

It would seem, then, that the greatest significance of evacuation to post-war Britain lay, ironically, in its failure as a policy. The government had been indicted from the first for failing to be active enough in carrying through its aims of relocating children in the countryside while simultaneously promoting their education. Working class families felt directly and keenly the failure of the policy. They were determined that better planning, and more efficiency in central government could guarantee their social and educational aspirations. At the same time, local officials and members of the central bureaucracy understood the meaning of the failure of evacuation; and they, too, were willing to accept more central planning than had been the case before 1939. The failures of a voluntary evacuation contrasted to the centralized successes of the government in prosecuting the war presented to post-war Britons an unmistakeable moral.

NOTES

1. Kenneth D. Brown, *The English Labour Movement, 1700-1951* (New York, 1982), p. 284; Henry Pelling, 'The 1945 General Election Reconsidered', *The Historical Journal*, vol. 23, no. 2 (1980), pp. 399-414.

2. Louis Heren, *Growing Up Poor in London* (London, 1973).

3. For a general study of felt deprivation, see W.G. Runciman, *Relative Deprivation and Social Justice* (Berkeley, 1966).

4. Roberts, *The Classic Slum*.

5. Madeline Kerr, *The People of Ship Street* (London, 1958).

6. Frank Parkin, 'Working-class Conservatives: A Theory of Political Deviance', *British Journal of Sociology*, vol. 18, no. 3 (September, 1967), pp. 278-290.

7. See, for example, Mark Benney,

A.P. Gray, and R.H. Pear, *How People Vote: A Study of Electoral Behavior in Greenwich* (London, 1956); and Eric A. Nordlinger, *The Working Class Tories* (London, 1967).

8. Frank Bealey, J. Blondel, and W.P. McCann, *Constituency Politics: A Study of Newcastle-under-Lyme* (London, 1955).

9. Roger Eatwell, *The 1945-1951 Labour Governments* (London, 1979), p. 43.

10. Addison, *The Road to 1945*, p. 17.

11. *Evacuation and the Churches: The Report of a Survey Committee Appointed by the Commission of the Churches for International Friendship and Social Responsibility* (London, 1941), p. 33.

12. *Ibid*., pp. 21-22.

13. *Ibid*., p. 54.

14. *Ibid*.

15. The following paragraphs are drawn from Gosden, *Education in the Second World War*, ch. 9; Titmuss, *Problems of Social Policy*, ch. XXV; and PRO Ed 50/222.

16. Hertfordshire Record Office, HCC 21/22, Education Committee, vol. 22, p. 233.

17. Titmuss, *Problems of Social Policy*, p. 510.

18. Sheila Ferguson and Hilde Fitzgerald, *Studies in the Social Services* (London, 1954), p. 183. My discussion of the wartime nurseries owes much to this useful work.

19. Denise Riley, *War in the Nursery* (London, 1983), p. 122.

20. Buckinghamshire Record Office, DC 18/1/42, Beaconsfield UDC Minutes of Evacuation Sub-Committee.

21. Shropshire Record Office, County Council Bundle System, Bundle 161, Box 22.

22. Gloucestershire Record Office, D372/9, Billeting and Evacuation, 1940.

23. Titmuss, *Problems of Social Policy*, pp. 364-68.

24. Hertfordshire Record Office, HCC21/23, Finance and General Purpose Sub-Committee, 31 March 1941, p. 140.

BIBLIOGRAPHY

This is not a complete bibliography: it contains merely the citations in the end notes for readers' convenience.

MANUSCRIPT COLLECTIONS

Bedfordshire Record Office
W/Ev/C/Z; W/Ev/C.W.V.4; W/Ev/3

Bristol Record Office
Evacuation Committee Minute Book,
1940-1945 School Logbooks

British Library Additional Manuscripts
Chuter-Ede Diary, Add Mss 59691, 59692

Buckinghamshire Record Office
Beaconsfield UDC Minutes of Evacuation Sub-Committee, DC 18/1/42

Churchill College, Cambridge
Hodsoll Papers

Cornwall Record Office
AD 336/21
B/T/86

Devon Record Office
AAP Evac., Box 11

Glouchestershire Record Office
C/CDa V 5/2
D 372/9, Billeting and Evacuation, 1940

Greater London Council History Library
C.R. Rawson, 'Pied Piper' manuscript

Greater London Record Office
CH/M/6/2; CH/M/6/4, Children's Handlist of LCC
EO/WAR/1/3 Evacuation Scheme, General Papers, May-July 1938
EO/WAR/1/4 Evacuation Scheme, General Papers, July-October 1938
EO/WAR/1/7, Evacuation Scheme, Anderson Report
EO/WAR/1/11, Evacuation Scheme, Correspondence with authorities in reception areas, April-August 1939
EO/WAR/1/48, Propaganda drive and possibility of compulsory evacuation, October 1940
EO/WAR/1/65, Billeting arrangements, January 1939-January 1940
EO/WAR/1/79, Plan IV, Results of Registration, March-June 1940
EO/WAR/1/81, Plan IV, Reports of Representatives at County Conferences, February-March 1940
EO/WAR/1/82, Plan IV, Billeting difficulties, January-June 1940
EO/WAR/1/83, Plan IV, Consultations with Teachers' Associations, February-November 1940
EO/WAR/1/84, Plan IV, Miscellaneous points, February-November 1940
EO/WAR/1/106, Plan V, Selective Evacuation
EO/WAR/1/127, 'Rivulet' Evacuation Program
EO/WAR/1/183, Plan IV, Policy, January-June 1940
EO/WAR/2/29, Springwell House Open-Air School
EO/WAR/3/5, Children returning to London, May-September 1940
EO/WAR/3/9, Re-opening of schools in London--General Papers, September 1939-February 1941
EO/WAR/3/12, Emergency Schools in London, November 1939-July 1940
EO/WAR/3/14, Re-imposition of compulsory attendance--General Policy, January 1940-July 1942

EO/WAR/3/18, Reports...during the period of 'fly-bomb' attacks, June-July 1944
EO/WAR/3/28, Damage and casualties at Sandhurst Road School, Catford, 25 January 1943
EO/WAR/3/43, Emergency Schools, General Principles, 1939
EO/WAR/4/3, Visits to reception areas
EO/WAR/5/1, School Diary of the Harbinger Infants School
EO/WAR/5/13, Wandsworth School

School Log Books
D.O. 1, Landford Road 'I', 1933-1950
D.O. 1, Peterborough 'M', 1940-1946
D.O. 5, Devons Road Emergency 'J.M'., 1942-1947
D.O. 6, Wickham Lane School Log Book, 'I', 1933-1959

Hampshire Record Office
Hampshire County Council Minutes, 16 November 1944

Hertfordshire Record Office
HCC 21/22, Education Committee
HCC 21/23, Finance and General Purpose Sub-Committee

Imperial War Museum
Elkus Collection
Ellison Memoirs, DS/Misc/49
LS. Box No. 77/50/1 Miss D.M. Hoyles

MacMaster University, Hamilton, Ontario, Canada
Vera Brittain Archives, 'Replies June 1940'

Mass Observation Archives, University of Sussex
Directive Replies, 1940
Topic Collection #5, Folder I/D, Folder I/E, Folder 2/A, Folder 2/K, Folder 2/K, Folder 2/L
War Diaries, C5282, M5376, N5382, 05390.0, W5220, W5229

New York Public Library
Ernst Papanek Papers, Box 11

Public Record Office, Kew
Cabinet Papers
CAB 46/22, CAB 46/23, CAB 73/1

Board of Education Papers
ED 10/246, ED 10/247, ED 10/248,
ED 50/196, ED 50/207, ED 50/212,
ED 50/222, ED 134/19, ED 134/73,
ED 134/74, ED 134/75, ED 134/77,
ED 134/256, ED 136/110, ED 136/111,
ED 136/112, ED 136/113, ED 136/114,
ED 136/116, ED 136/125, ED 136/205,
ED 136/212, ED 136/665, ED 138/26,
ED 138/34, ED 138/35, ED 138/36,
ED 138/50

Ministry of Housing and Local Government Papers
HLG 7/74, HLG 7/75, HLG 7/76,
HLG 7/82, HLG 7/90, HLG 7/101,
HLG 7/114, HLG 7/322, HLG 7/334,
HLG 68/5

Home Office Papers
HO 45/16634, HO 45/17635,
HO 45/17636, HO 45/18163,
HO 45/18164, HO 45/18716,
HO 45/19065, HO 45/230811,
HO 186/342, HO 186/343

Ministry of Health Papers
MH 79/86, MH 79/87

Shropshire Record Office
County Council Bundle System
Evacuation 161, Box 22
Evacuation 161A, Box 21
Evacuation 162, Box 23

Trinity College, Cambridge
R.A. Butler Papers

Warwickshire Record Office,
CR 1557/152;
CR 1560/65

Wiltshire Record Office
Clerks 273/1 WAR
Clerks 273/3/46C

Yale University Archives
A. Sydney Lovett Papers, Box 55
YRG 6B, Box 2

Yale University Medical Library
Diary of John Fulton, vol. XIV

PARLIAMENTARY PUBLICATIONS

Hansard's Parliamentary Debates, 1937, 1938, 1939, 1940

Report of Committee on Evacuation (London, 1938), Cmd. 5837

Report...into the Accident at Bethnal Green Tube Station Shelter (London, 1943), Cmd. 6583

PERIODICALS AND NEWSPAPERS

Birmingham Post

Daily Express

Daily Herald

Daily Telegraph

East End News

East London Advertiser

Education

Evening News

Faringdon Advertiser

The Journal of Education

The London Teacher

Manchester Guardian

Newbury Weekly News

New Statesman

News Chronicle

North Berks Herald

Reading Mercury

Reading Standard

The Schoolmaster

The Spectator

The Times

Times Educational Supplement

Windsor Express

Yorkshire Post

SECONDARY WORKS

Addison, Paul. *The Road to 1945: British Politics and the Second World War* (London, 1975)

Bailey, Anthony. *America Lost and Found* (New York, 1980)

Banks, Olive. *Parity and Prestige in English Secondary Education* (London, 1955)

Baring, Norah. *A Friendly Hearth* (London, 1946)

Bealey, Frank, Blondel, J., and McCann, W.P. *Constituency Politics: A Study of Newcastle-under-Lyme* (London, 1955)

Benney, Mark, Gray, A.P., and Pear, R.H. *How People Vote: A Study of Electoral Behavior in Greenwich* (London, 1956)

Body, Alfred H. *Children in Flight* (London, 1940)

Brittain, Vera. _England's Hour_ (New York, 1941)

Brittain, Vera. _Testament of Experience: An Autobiographical Story of the Years 1925-1950_ (New York, 1981)

Brock, M. Dorothy. _An Unusual Happening: The Story of The Mary Datchelor Girls School in Evacuation, September 1939-May 1945_ (Privately printed; no date)

Brown, Kenneth D. _The English Labour Movement, 1700-1951_ (New York, 1982)

Busby, William H. _Our Evacuees: A Reminiscence_ (London, 1941)

Butler, Lord. _The Art of Memory_ (London, 1982)

Butler, Lord. _The Art of the Possible_ (Penquin Books, 1975)

Colvin, Ian. _The Chamberlain Cabinet_ (London, 1971)

Cooper, Diana. _Trumpets from the Steep_ (London, 1940)

Cosgrave, Patrick. _R.A. Butler: An English Life_ (London, 1980)

Dale, H.E. _The Higher Civil Service of Great Britain_ (Oxford, 1941)

Dent, H.C. _Education in Transition_ (London, 1944)

Despert, J. Louise. _Preliminary Report on Children's_ Reactions to the War (n.p., 1942)

Donoghue, Bernard and Jones, G.W. _Herbert Morrison_: Portrait of a Politician (London, 1973)

Eatwell, Roger. _The 1945-1951 Labour Governments_ (London, 1979)

Education, Ministry of. _Education, 1900-1950_ (London, 1951)

Evacuation and the Churches: The Report of a Survey Committee Appointed by the Commission of the Churches for International Friendship and Social Responsibility (London, 1941)

Fenwick, I.G.K. _The Comprehensive School, 1944-1970: The Politics of Secondary School Reorganization_ (London, 1976)

Ferguson, Sheila and Fitzgerald, Hilde. _Studies in the Social Services_ (London, 1954)

Floud, J.E. _et. al._ _Social Class and Educational Opportunity_ (London, 1957)

Forbes-Robertson, Diana and Straus, Roger W., Jr. (eds.), _War Letters from Britain_ (New York, 1941)

Gaunt, H.C.A. _Two Exiles: Being a Record of Malvern College During the War_ (London, 1946)

Gosden, P.H.J.H. _How They Were Taught_ (New York, 1969)

Gosden, P.H.J.H. _Education in the Second World War_ (London, 1976)

Gould, Stephen Jay. _The Mismeasure of Man_ (New York, 1981)

Graves, Charles. _Women in Green_ (London, 1948)

Grunfeld, Judith. _Shefford: The Story of a Jewish School Community in Evacuation, 1939-1945_ (London, 1980)

Heren, Louis. _Growing Up Poor in London_ (London, 1973)

Holmes, Colin. _Anti-Semitism in British Society, 1976-1939_ (London, 1979)

Huxley, Elspeth. _Atlantic Ordeal: The Story of Mary Cornish_ (London, 1941)

J.C.H.T. Clifton at Bude and Butcombe: The Story of a School in Evacuation (Bristol, 1945)

Jackson, Carlton. Who Will Take Our Children? (London, 1985)

Jesse, F. Tennyson and Harwood, H.M. Letters Written to America (August 1939-July 1940) (London, 1940)

Johnson, Franklyn Arthur. Defense by Committee: The British Committee of Imperial Defense, 1935-1959 (London, 1960)

Jones, Thomas. A Diary with Letters, 1931-1950 (London, 1954)

Kelsall, R.K. Higher Civil Servants in Britain (London, 1955)

Kerr, Madeline. The People of Ship Street (London, 1958)

Leakey, J.H. School Errant: The Story of the War-Time Adventures of Dulwich College Preparatory School (London, 1951)

Lebzelter, Gisela C. Political Anti-Semitism in England, 1919-1939 (London, 1978)

Leon, Philip et al. Evacuation: A National Opportunity (n.p., 1940)

London County Council. Interim Report of the County Medical Officer of Health and School Medical Officer for the Year 1939 (n.p., n.d.)

London County Council. Standard of Attainment in London Elementary Schools (London, 1943)

Lowndes, G.A.N. Silent Social Revolution (Oxford, 1969), 2nd ed.

MacInnes, C.M. Bristol at War (London, 1962)

MacLaine, Ian. Ministry of Morale (London, 1979)

MacLean, Meta. The Singing Ship: An Odyssey of Evacuee Children (Sydney, 1941)

Marwick, Arthur. War and Social Change in the Twentieth Century (London, 1974)

Marwick, Arthur. The Home Front: The British and the Second World War (London, 1976)

Medical Officers of School Association. Annual Proceedings and Report, No. 14 (1939-43)

National Federation of Women's Institutes, Town Children Through Country Eyes (Dorking, Surrey, 1940)

Nordlinger, Eric A. The Working Class Tories (London, 1967)

O'Brien, Terence H. Civil Defense (London, 1955)

Orlands, Harold. Stevenage: A Sociological Study of a New Town (London, 1976: Kraus Reprint)

Padley, Richard and Cole, Margaret (eds.), Evacuation Survey: A Report to the Fabian Society (London, 1940)

Parkinson, Michael. The Labour Party and the Organization of Education, 1918-1965 (London, 1970)

Pelham, Angela. The Young Ambassadors (London, 1944)

Riley, Denise. War in the Nursery (London, 1983)

Roberts, Robert. The Classic Slum: Salford Life in the First Quarter of the Century (Manchester, 1971)

Runciman, W.G. Relative Deprivation and Social Justice (Berkeley, 1966)

Shakespeare, Geoffrey. Let Candles Be Brought In (London, 1949)

Simon, Brian. The Politics of Educational Reform (London, 1974)

Stacy, Margaret. Tradition and Change: A Study of Banbury (Oxford, 1960)

Taylor, A.J.P. A Personal History (New York, 1983)

Titmuss, Richard. Problems of Social Policy (London, 1976: Kraus Reprint)

Vernon, Betty D. Ellen Wilkinson, 1891-1947 (London, 1982)

Wersky, Gary. The Visible College: The Collective Biography of British Scientific Socialists of the 1930's (New York, 1978)

Wheeler-Bennett, John W. John Anderson: Viscount Waverley (London, 1962)

Williams, W.M. The Sociology of an English Village: Gosforth (London, 1956)

Winnington Women's Institute. Winnington: The History of a Bedfordshire Village (n.p., 1946)

ARTICLES

Amir, Yehuda. 'Contact Hypothesis in Ethnic Relations', Psychological Bulletin, Vol 71, No 5 (May 1969), 319-42

Bodman, Frank. 'Child Psychiatry in War Time Britain', Journal of Educational Psychology, Vol XXXV, No 5 (May 1944), 293-301

Chambers, Rosalind C. 'A Study of Three Voluntary Organizations', in Social Mobility in Britain, ed. D.V. Glass (London, 1954)

Crossick, Geoffrey. 'The Emergence of the Lower Middle Class in Britain: A Discussion', in The Lower Middle Class in Britain,

1870-1914, ed. Geoffrey Crossick (New York, 1977)

Davies, M. 'Education in the Second World War: The Preparation of an Official History', Journal of Educational Administration and History, Vol VIII, No 1 (January 1976), 51-55

Dean, D.W. 'Problems of the Conservative Sub-Committee on Education, 1941-45', Journal of Educational Administration and History, Vol III, No 1 (December 1970), 16-37

Jones, Greta. 'Eugenics and Social Policy Between the Wars', The Historical Journal, Vol 25, No 3 (1982) 717-28

Laqueur, Thomas W. 'Working Class Demand and the Growth of English Elementary Education, 1750-1850', in Schooling and Society: Studies in the History of Education, ed. Lawrence Stone (Baltimore, 1976)

Lowe, R.A. 'Eugenicists, Doctors, and the Quest for National Efficiency: An Educational Crusade, 1900-1939', History of Education, Vol 8, No 4 (1979) 292-306

Owen, A.D.K. 'The Great Evacuation', The Political Quarterly, Vol Xl (1940)

Parkin, Frank. 'Working-class Conservatives: A Theory of Political Deviance', British Journal of Sociology, Vol 18, No 3 (September 1967), 278-90

Pelling, Henry. 'The 1945 General Election Reconsidered', The Historical Journal, Vol 23, No 2 (1980), 399-414

Pritchard, Rosemary and Rosenzweig, Saul. 'The Effects of War Stress upon Childhood and Youth', The Journal of Abnormal and Social Psychology Vol 37, No 3 (July 1942), 329-44

Rubinstein, David. 'Ellen Wilkinson Re-Considered', *History Workshop*, Vol 7 (Spring 1979), 161-69

Turner, C.M. 'Sociological Approaches to the History of Education', *British Journal of Educational Studies*, Vol XVII, No 2 (June 1969), 146-65

Valentine, C.W. 'Editorial Note on Evacuation Investigations',*British Journal of Educational Psychology*, Vol XI (1941)

Vernon, P.E. 'Psychological Effects of Air-Raids', *Journal of Abnormal and Social Psychology*, Vol 36, No 4 (October 1941), 457-76

Wallace, R.G. 'The Origins and Authorship of the 1944 Education Act', *History of Education*, Vol 10, No 4 (1981), 283-90

Wolf, Katherine M. 'Evacuation of Children in Wartime', *Psychoanalytic Study of the Child*, Vol 1 (1945), 389-404

UNPUBLISHED DISSERTATION

Burgevin, Jules David. 'Politics and Education: Case Study of a Pressure Group, The National Association of Labour Teachers, 1927-1951' (Syracuse University Ph.D. dissertation 1969)

INDEX